HEALING
THE WOUNDS
OF CHILDHOOD

HEALING THE WOUNDS OF CHILDHOOD

**A Recovery Guide for Adult Children
of Dysfunctional Families**

Dennis J. McGuire, Ph.D.

A PERIGEE BOOK

Perigee Books
are published by
The Putnam Publishing Group
200 Madison Avenue
New York, NY 10016

Library of Congress Cataloging-in-Publication Data

McGuire, Dennis J.
Healing the wounds of childhood: a recovery guide for adult children
of dysfunctional families/by Dennis J. McGuire
p. cm.
Includes bibliographical references.
ISBN 0-399-51615-8
1. Adult children of dysfunctional families—Rehabilitation.
2. Adult children of dysfunctional families—Case studies.
3. Twelve-step programs. I. Title.
RC455.4.F3M39 1990   90-36310 CIP
616.85′2—dc20

Printed in the United States of America
1 2 3 4 5 6 7 8 9 10

CONTENTS

CONTENTS

CONTENTS

INTRODUCTION

This book has been written for individuals who feel that the families they grew up in did not provide them with the nurturing, guidance, and love that they need for the enjoyment of life as fully functioning, healthy, and mature adults. It is for people whose childhood experiences were more structured by neglect and abuse than by nurturing and love. For some time I have been searching for a book that would provide helpful guidance as to how a person gets into, goes through, and comes out of the process of recovering from such a childhood. Not having found it, I decided to create a book that would provide this kind of guidance.

My own life, both as a career consultant and as an individual struggling with the personality disorders wrought by a dysfunctional childhood, has forced me to face the emotionally painful issues that recovery entails. In guiding individuals through the career decision process, the differences between those who experienced supportive childhoods and those who were neglected or abused are glaringly apparent. The latter suffer from chronic anxiety, patterns of underemployment, and negative self-images. I, too, faced personal torments, and at one point lost complete control over my own thoughts and behaviors. A few years ago, I found myself obsessing uncontrollably about doing away with a colleague whom I blamed for the problems I was having in relating to others. I then decided to seek help. A psychiatrist informed me about meetings conducted by adults who had grown up in dysfunctional families, and I date the beginning of my recovery from the time I first participated in such meetings. But recovery raised a new set of issues that I needed to address.

What, for example, is the process of reparenting yourself, of healing the wounds of childhood, and of growing to adult fulfillment? For those who have embarked on the journey of recovery this book describes the experience of the recovery process, and the destination of the journey. Individuals on this journey often ask with burning impatience, "Where am I going?" "How close to, or far from, my destination am I?" "Where am I, and what progress, if any, am I making?"

This burning impatience is experienced as part of the recovery process itself. Because recovery is a process it takes time. A person in pain experiences time as infinitely longer than he does when calm. And time is life. So a person who is in the process of recovery really wants to know the answers to these questions. If you are such a person, you need some reassurance that the time and energy you are spending is worth it. You need a good map that shows where you are going on the journey of recovery and what to expect on the way.

My recovery from an emotionally chaotic childhood has included professional and service activities in addition to those personal to me. Founding the *ACOA* [Adult Children of Alcoholics] *Recovery Bulletin,* starting a support group meeting, and participating in the design and conduct of retreats involved interacting with other recovering adults. Such interactions entailed meetings, confrontations, agreements, disagreements, and letting go of my biases in the consensus-building process. Recovery, I have found, is not a process shaped by my preconceptions, but one with its own inherent laws of cause and effect.

My professional training in educational psychology and experience as a support group facilitator and career consultant have brought me into intimate contact with the personal struggles of many individuals. The most universally valid fact I have observed in working with hundreds of adults in recovery is that it is extremely difficult for them to have a realistic idea of what the recovery process is.

Other developmental processes are well defined, and even institutionalized. If, for example, you decide to get a college degree, you have a specific goal to accomplish. The college you attend will provide you with a degree program that is a sequence of tasks that must be performed over a specified period of time. It will state what courses you must take to complete your work for the degree. In each course the professor will tell you what assignments you are to complete, and will evaluate your performance. You will be graded on each assignment and for each course. After about four years of such work you will be awarded the degree you set out to get. There will be a graduation ceremony to commemorate the event, and you can celebrate with family and friends, and receive their congratulations.

Every step of the way in this process is clear-cut and well defined by tradition. It is defined by others who have gone through the process before you and who are in a position to set up a program that is officially recognized as valid. But in the recovery process you will find that things are not so clearly defined. You will have to make decisions on your own. You will have to formulate your own program. You will have to evaluate your own performance. But you may not feel adequate to do this. After all, you are beginning to acknowledge your inadequacies about judging your own behaviors. Moreover, you may see others who have pronounced themselves recovered or healed, and yet you perceive that they have merely exchanged one set of dysfunctional behaviors for another. You may feel afraid of falling into the same trap.

This book provides you with a practical guide to the recovery process. It consolidates the information available in the literature on recovery and organizes it in the sequence of stages through which you must pass. This book is unique because it presents this information in a sequential order. Its central focus is that you must pass through a specific number of stages in recovery. Each stage takes time, and the experiences you will have in each stage can be anticipated. This book presents this material through the daily life experiences of people working toward their "graduation" in recovery. Of course, growing does not end with attaining mature adulthood any more than learning ends with the attainment of a college degree. But the goal of recovery is the attainment of mature adulthood, and this book describes clearly how this can be accomplished.

You can expect to experience certain things over the next several years of your life. The recovery process is lengthy, but it has a beginning, a middle, and an end. You can get stuck along the way, and you can drop out for a while (until the pain brings you back). This book explains what to do at each stage of your recovery.

The practical nature of this book stems from its emphasis on specific behavioral transactions that people experience in their families, personal friendships, social relationships, jobs, and careers. The predictable sequence of expected patterns in recovery is described in terms that you can use to evaluate your progress. Use this book as a guide to your program of recovery. Use it to evaluate yourself, and to determine how far along you are toward your "graduation." While other books provide general information about the issues faced in recovery, this book offers a practical way to focus your energy on exactly what is occurring and on what you should concentrate at each stage of your recovery program.

There are a number of excellent books on the issues of recovery (see the Bibliography). This book is the first to describe recovery issues and concepts as an appropriate and manageable sequence of daily life experiences that you can expect to occur.

That is why this book has been put together not just by me but by the many people who have contributed the knowledge and insights derived from their experience. These are people recovering from childhoods that were experienced as traumatic. For one reason or another, their families did not provide them with the encouragement and growth-inducing love that their young hearts needed. Their childhoods were consistently lacking in this love, attention, and nurturing. It is this lack of healthy child-centeredness that identifies their families as dysfunctional.

Often adults whose parents were not physically abusive, alcoholic, or verbally critical wonder about the nature of their family's dysfunction. Was it an identifiable mental illness? Was the parent manic-depressive? Schizophrenic? Psychotic? Or was it that the parents themselves came from nonnurturing families? Sometimes people feel it is necessary to have the right label to convince themselves their family was dysfunctional. But any family in which the children, in order to survive physically, mentally, emotionally, and spiritually, must adapt to the psychological maladjustments of their parents is dysfunctional.

For example, I remember spending a lot of time at home with my mother when I was three and four years old. I can see her on her hands and knees dusting the table in our dining room. I would come to her and say I wanted to help. It looked like a game that I would enjoy playing. If I had a rag I could do what my mom was doing. With a ferocious hatred and disgust in her voice she would shout, "The best thing you could do to help me is to leave me alone!"

As an isolated event this would not amount to trauma, but as a pattern in the way she related to me it was just that. I heard my mother saying she would be relieved of a tremendous burden if I would just disappear.

She would also threaten me regularly by saying, "Wait till your father gets home!" Since my father had begun beating me when I was about four years old, this was not a threat to be taken lightly. So I spent many days living in a state of terror, and grew up with a deep sense of shame.

When, as an adult in recovery, I felt the need for a book like this, and realized I would have to create it, I knew it would be necessary to go to many of the people from such families who are sincerely devoted to the process of recovery. I have interviewed them for specific behavioral accounts about how they see themselves changing while on the journey of recovery. I have learned about the changes that occur as a result of coping with the pain they feel, of dealing with their emotional issues, of constantly searching for relief, and possibly joy, and relentlessly trying to be the people that they truly feel they are meant to be.

Herbert Gravitz and Julie Bowden are therapists who have identified the stages of recovery through which their adult children clients must progress. The people I interviewed for this work demonstrate the necessity of these stages. The purpose of this book is to show you how this is actually being accomplished by people. They relate stories that show how their beliefs, attitudes, and behaviors have changed from dysfunctional to healthy. Many specific incidents illustrate each stage in the recovery process. If you have committed yourself to this process you can see what direction your recovery can take by reading about these changes.

HEALING
THE WOUNDS
OF CHILDHOOD

CHAPTER 1

THE CHARACTERISTICS OF ADULT CHILDREN

Growing up in a dysfunctional family engenders patterns of attitudes and behaviors that are widespread and typical. Parents who cannot find serenity within themselves as they mature through adulthood inevitably project their feelings of emotional inadequacy and spiritual emptiness onto their children.

Blame and Denial: The Roots of the Adult Child Personality Disorder

In healthy families where the parents are experiencing intimacy and their own growth, they may at times blame their children for specific undesirable behaviors. But if your family was unhealthy and your parents were experiencing emotional isolation, personal stagnation, and despair, they constantly blamed you for their own unhappiness. This blaming made you feel that you were a bad person, a person who, because there is something wrong with you, is responsible for the misery of your parents. At the same time your parents denied that there was anything wrong with themselves. They may even have avowed that their family was better than most others. In its simplest terms the disorder of unhealthy families can be called a syndrome of blame and denial.

Blame

Through blame you were criticized, scolded, and perhaps beaten or incested. Thus you were being told that you were to blame for your parents' unhappiness, frustration, and low self-esteem. If you tried to express how you felt about the situation, you were intimidated into suppressing your feelings or told there was nothing wrong. The reality you perceived was denied by your parents. In its place was substituted a myth such as the belief that your family was in some way better than others, that others were pretending to be happy, and/or that yours was different from others because it was special in some way. Family loyalty is a strong instinct and functions to support whatever myth replaces the acknowledgement of a reality that seems basically unacceptable. With such blame and denial dysfunctional self-images developed in you. You have carried such images, along with their beliefs, attitudes, and behaviors, into adulthood.

Elizabeth, one of the people I interviewed, spoke of the blame she received as a child. Her experience illustrates the effect of constant blaming by a dysfunctional parent. Today she is a successful forty-six-year-old psychotherapist, but as a child she was beaten repeatedly by her mentally ill mother. The constant blaming by her mother made her feel responsible for her mother's unhappiness. Yet she was powerless to make her mother happy. She believes that "the powerlessness itself was terrible, but later on, what compounded the feeling was that I was told I was responsible for the maintenance of good feelings in the household. My mother said that if I had cleaned the house like she told me to she wouldn't have had to beat me." To survive this situation with some vestige of personal identity, Elizabeth accepted the belief that her inadequacy was the cause of her mother's continued unhappiness. This led to the attitude that she was responsible for her mother's behavior. She acted this out by postponing play until her household chores were done perfectly. Since they were never done perfectly, one of the consequences she suffered was never having time for play, and not learning how to play.

The self-image Elizabeth developed was that she was to blame, or held responsible, for her mother's unhappiness. She did not know that her mother's unhappiness was due to her own mental illness. She did not know that it was her mother's responsibility to provide her with nurturing love. She was told that her mother's mood depended on her performance of household chores and other duties, and that she would be punished if this performance was not perfect. She did not know that it was abusive of her mother to demand such perfection. She thought that if she tried hard enough she might someday get it right, be perfect, and make her mother happy. She internalized the blame bestowed on her by her mother, who was in denial of her responsibility for her own happiness.

Denial

Extensive studies have been conducted on the phenomenon of denial. It has been found to be the expected first reaction of humans to bad news, failure, and the whole spectrum of personal and business disasters. In this sense it is a normal reaction. Upon first hearing that one has terminal cancer, for example, one can be expected to react with denial. Typical denials could include "Nobody in my family has cancer, therefore I don't have it"; "There must be some mistake"; or "I'm sure it's not that serious." Therapists have learned that treatment begins with getting through the denial reaction.

Getting through the denial reaction involves accepting the undesirable situation as reality. For example, individuals accept that they really do have cancer that has been diagnosed as terminal. They then talk out all their fears of the consequences of this reality with trusted others. They feel and express their anger in nondamaging ways. They take responsibility for the situation, and determine what can be done about it. For example, they can resign themselves to death, seek other medical opinions on the diagnosis, find a support group program for people with such a condition, look for holistic cures, and so forth. This process depends on a willingness to accept an undesirable reality as fact. Denial is the defense mechanism that relieves the individual of the responsibility for taking effective action.

Denial is far different from positive imagining. Research with cancer patients at Yale University Medical Center found that those in denial died faster than those who took a realistic attitude toward their condition. Deniers insist, "I'm fine, everything is wonderful," when, states Dr. Bernie Siegel, "you know they have cancer, their spouses have run off, their children are drug addicts, and the house has just burned down." The research he cites indicates that denial "exhausts the immune system because the immune system is confused by the mixed messages." People who accept the reality of their condition with courage have a better chance of surviving because they participate in fighting it.

When a dysfunctional parent mistreated you and claimed that their behavior was justified by your misconduct, that parent denied the real nature of his or her unhappiness. It was easier to blame you than to take responsibility for their own attitudes and behaviors. Blame and denial work together. They are the twin manifestations of an individual's inability or refusal to take responsibility for their own condition in life.

But as a child you did not know what therapists know, and in your unhealthy family your personality was shaped by your parents' lifestyle of denial. This denial is pathologically enduring. Such parental denial of feelings and events created self-doubt in you. It worked against your learning about yourself and the development of your potential for self-love.

The testimony of another contributor to this book illustrates the effects of denial. As a child Candy knew there was something wrong with what was going on in her family, but the reality she perceived was constantly denied. Now in her thirties, she comes from a family that owns a successful restaurant in her native town. Her alcoholic father would often come home "that way" and give her a look that served notice she had better "shut down." When she asked whether that was normal her mother would say, "Nothing's wrong. Dad's just tired, don't worry about it." "As a result I questioned my own feelings," she says. "As things progressed I questioned my own sanity. If they are always telling me that nothing is wrong, then I must be the crazy one."

Denial is further served when the family appears successful and wholesome to the community. A beautiful house or expensive car, the oldest child's success in school, and his or her "maturity" at a young age, the entire family praying piously in church every Sunday, fabled stories about the family's "successes," memberships and active participation in social clubs, and other superficially acceptable activities all function to hide the devastating hopelessness at the core of the dysfunctional family. When, as a child, you perceived the discrepancies in your parents' behaviors, you may have wondered who was crazy: "Am I crazy? Are they crazy? Is the whole world crazy?" Whichever of these alternatives may be "right," it was hardly reassuring to you. Denial created an environment of anxious insecurity.

As a result of these experiences you grew to adulthood feeling that you are to blame for, and therefore responsible for, the miseries of your companions, the problems of your employers, and the faults of any situation in which you find yourself. You feel responsible for the situations and may try to fix them.

The lifelong experience of denial leaves you guessing about what should be normal expectations. If, from an early age, you had been told and had understood that the chaos in your family was due to your parents' dysfunctions, your confidence in your own perceptions would be validated. But who was going to tell you this, particularly at times when you were being traumatized? Certainly your abusive parent was not going to make such an admission. Their denial caused the abuse. The other parent was not going to support you because they coped by denying that anything was wrong, except your "childish" perception.

Thus you came to adulthood unable to rely on your instincts in making decisions about who is a suitable friend or spouse, what working conditions are fair, and, in general, how to behave. You may feel in control of your life, but spontaneity and joy are displaced by anger. You may be accomplished and successful in your work, but still feel empty. You may feel victimized by circumstances, but confused as to how your decisions and actions bring about the painful consequences you experience.

Healthy vs. Unhealthy Development in Childhood

A great deal has been written about dysfunctional families and the unhealthy effects of blame and denial on their children. I think it is appropriate at this point to consider what constitutes a healthy upbringing. I say "healthy" rather than "normal" because it may very well be normal, in our society, to be a member of a dysfunctional family. After researching this issue thoroughly, Terry Gorsky stated in 1988 that as many as 80 percent of the families in contemporary America are dysfunctional.

If you wish to be a healthy human being, some important questions to be considered are: Do you want to feel secure with your own values, and not need the approval of others? Do you want to enjoy intimacy without the fear of abandonment? Do you want to contribute to the community of people with whom you are involved? Do you want to feel, as you grow older, that your life is worthwhile, and that it can serve as a role model for others? These are the questions this book is concerned with, not from a philosophical point of view, but from the practical perspective of everyday living.

Since as a survivor of a dysfunctional family system you are attempting to experience the growth you did not have as a child, it makes sense to outline the growth process that you missed. In functional and dysfunctional family systems the children and adults proceed through stages of growth and development or progressive deterioration, respectively. The healthy results that can be expected at each stage, as well as

The Stages of Normal Growth and Development Showing Healthy and Unhealthy Results (Adapted from Erik Erikson)

HEALTHY	UNHEALTHY
FIRST YEAR	
The infant experiences the world as nurturing, reliable and trustworthy. He develops the capacity for intimacy.	The infant does not have a warm nurturing experience, and the capacity for intimacy will be correspondingly impaired.
SECOND YEAR	
A warm, secure relationship between the child and parents helps the child develop a feeling of being in control of herself, combined with pleasant, self-confident feelings.	The child develops feelings of shame and doubt about herself and her body.

TWO TO FIVE The child learns to live as a member of the family. Conscience is developed and the usual defense mechanisms are used to deal with normal or abnormal anxieties.

The child feels able to do many exciting things and can take the initiative. The child develops confidence in his abilities but with his impulses under adequate control.	The child feels that others will be angry with or even destroy him if he does what he wants. The child feels frightened and guilty.

FIVE OR SIX TO TEN The development of self-esteem is a central issue. Gradually the child gets an idea of her capacities and limitations. Standards of social behavior are further refined and ideas of right and wrong elaborated. The personality attributes that a child has acquired by the end of this period tend to persist into adult life.

The child learns the basic skills and knowledge and, as a result, comes to enjoy personal satisfaction, recognition, and the chance to relate to other people.	The child develops a sense of inadequacy and inferiority.

ADOLESCENCE Adolescents often belong to groups that offer support in the transition from family member to self-sufficient person.

At the end of adolescence the young person knows who she is and is confident in making this identity known to the world. By late adolescence the individual should be able to enter into relationships involving tender affection as well as sexual feelings.	Role confusion develops. Emotional turmoil is experienced as the norm. Defensiveness interferes with sharing affection, and sexuality is confused with intimacy.
YOUNG ADULT The person is now ready for intimacy with others in close relationships, including sexual union.	Failure at this stage results in isolation.
ADULT The person contributes to the establishing and guiding of the next generation (not necessarily through parenthood).	The individual stagnates and experiences personal impoverishment.
FINAL STAGE: The person's life experiences are integrated, people and things taken care of, triumphs and disappointments accepted.	The person experiences despair and feels the fear of death, owing to the sense that time is now too short to live a worthwhile life.

the unhealthy counterparts, have been described by Erik Erikson.

Erikson emphasizes that parental actions in caring for a child convey meaningful messages that are either positive or negative. At each stage of growth in life messages are incorporated into one's experience of life that shape one's personality. In early childhood the messages come to an individual primarily from parents. Later stages of growth involve messages from school, work situations, church, and other social institutions, as well as peer groups. The parental influence is crucial to how the child interprets the messages received at school from peers and adults.

In the first year of life different parents may appear to give the same degree of care to their infants, and yet their attitudes can convey very different messages. The meaning conveyed by a healthy parent during your first year of life could have been "You are important to me, I'm glad you're here." This would instill feelings of trust in you as an infant, and develop your ability to experience intimacy. Your unhealthy parent's message may have been "What a pain in the neck you are. I wish you weren't my responsibility." The result was a sense of distrust in you as an infant, and a corresponding impairment of your ability to experience intimacy.

The second year of life involves toilet training and weaning activities. "I'm here to assist you become more autonomous in your bodily functioning" is the message of a healthy parent. This would have encouraged a sense of autonomy in you as a child. "Shame on you, look what you've done" is quite another message. The expected result would be a sense of shame developing in you.

Nurturing messages at ages two to five can be summarized as "You are worthy as a human being and therefore must act

28

in a responsible way." This is unconditional love, and would encourage the sense of initiative in you as a child. "Your worth as a human being depends on doing right and avoiding wrong" is the message of conditional love. It created a sense of guilt in you.

Ages five to ten involve schooling experiences reinforced by the family system. "You are doing well, it's fun to work with you, and we know we can depend on you" is the message encouraging the healthy development of a sense of industry. Its counterpart is "You are doing poorly, you are inadequate, and your work is mediocre. We don't expect much from you." To the extent you received this message you developed a sense of inferiority.

During adolescence, with the bodily changes and growth started in puberty, the messages relate to a growing social identity. "You fit in with the crowd and your group is a socially acceptable one" is a positive message. Such a message would help you as an adolescent to form your own sense of identity. "You don't fit in, and the people you associate with are losers" is its opposite. To the extent you got this message it developed role confusion in you as an adolescent. In 1981 Sharon Wegscheider-Cruse, a dysfunctional-family counselor, described the typical roles taken on by children in such families as the family hero, the scapegoat, the lost child, and the mascot.

As adulthood arrives the key issue is intimacy. Intimacy may or may not involve sex. To the extent that sex in a love relationship is experienced as compulsive, it interferes with true intimacy. Intimacy may be experienced between friends, business partners, fellow workers, team members, support group participants, and, in general, in any relationship in which people are learning to understand and appreciate themselves and one another. As Erikson stated, intimacy involves the building of trust and partnership within a framework of mutually expressed and received commitment.

The message of success with intimacy between young adult lovers is "You can deal with the hostilities and potential rages caused by the fancied and real differences between the sexes. You do this by working to achieve mutual sexual gratifications and partnership satisfactions." The opposite message is "You gratify yourself sexually in ways that you must keep secret, and no one who knows your secrets would choose to be intimate with you." As a result you will feel a growing sense of isolation and the pain of loneliness.

If you are a healthy adult who lives and works within intimate relationships your society can communicate to you, "You have a vested interest in guiding the younger generation. Your contribution is needed." When intimacy has proved elusive, on the other hand, you may get the message, "You can indulge yourself and be content with your self-centered lifestyle." This attitude results in personal stagnation.

At the final stage of life a positive message is, "Given your gifts and the times you live in, you are a good example of an emotionally and spiritually balanced human being." This is the growth experience of ego integrity that you can feel as a maturing adult. Its negative counterpart is, "It's too late for you to straighten out your life. You are disgusted with many things in your life but time is running out. You have missed the boat, and there is no other way to go." As a result you will experience a sense of despair.

Finally, a look at the summary of growth stages shows an important feature of the family system. In a healthy family the adults are experiencing intimacy, making their contribution, and growing in personal integrity, while their children develop trust, security, and a socially responsible self-esteem. In the unhealthy family the adults are experiencing isolation, stagnation, and despair, while their children develop distrust, self-doubt, and feelings of inadequacy.

Recovery from Unhealthy Parenting

As a survivor of an unhealthy family you have to learn as an adult what you were not allowed to learn as a child. Most of what you learned as a child about yourself and relating to others—distrust, self-doubt, and feelings of inadequacy—has to be unlearned. For you, the process of growing from a child in an adult's body to an adult involves the pain of self-recrimination when progress is interrupted by regression, the pain of anger that has been bottled up for decades, and the pain of learning by trial and error when many of the trials result in errors. You may have an anger over not having had a healthy childhood and, as a recovering adult, you must grieve this loss. You must also work through reexperiencing, processing, and letting go of the unresolved emotional issues from the past. This is part of the process known as recovery.

The pain you feel is the aching discrepancy between what you consciously want and what your inner *true self* needs, such as a healthy self-esteem, shared commitments of trust with others, peace of mind, a joyful acceptance and sharing of love, and fun. As this pain gets more and more unbearable you can be drawn to whatever will alleviate it, such as alcohol, drugs, compulsive sex and/or eating, codependent love, excessive work, and other anaesthetically effective medications or activities. On the other hand, alleviation can be found in the changes in perceptions, beliefs, attitudes, and behaviors that are more aligned with your inner *true self.*

Your question "How long will my recovery take?" can best be answered if it is understood as a cry of pain. A plausible answer may be "From three to six years, depending on the nature of your dysfunctions, the quality of your therapy and support system, and your desire for personal growth." A truer answer is "Your pain can diminish dramatically as self-alienation is replaced by self-acceptance, and despair by hope." As you come to appreciate your pain as a way in which your *true self* communicates with your conscious self, the pain comes to function as a guide for the changes that are needed in your life.

The Process of Recovery

If you missed a full portion of nurturing love, from the intimacy of the first year of your life to your socialization in adolescence, you must experience it now if you are to recover. If you are to change from an individual who is alienated by your dysfunctional beliefs, attitudes, and behavior patterns, you have to experience nurturing love. There is no other way. You cannot do it "on your own." To change from a distrusting cynic to a joyful truster, you need the supportive love of others who truly understand and accept you. Many experiences of such supportive love are needed to fashion and complete your recovery over time. Your process of recovery is your process of growing up.

Recovery for adult children of dysfunctional families usually involves personal therapy and participation in support meetings of groups such as Adult Children of Alcoholics (ACOA or ACA), Codependents Anonymous (CODA), or similar groups.

Adult Children of Alcoholics, for example, is a national

grass-roots program that is modeled on the Twelve Step recovery program pioneered by Alcoholics Anonymous. At meetings that are well run, adults from all kinds of dysfunctional families express their thoughts and feelings about themselves and how their lives are progressing. Some prefer to listen as others share. Two-way conversation and advice giving are not allowed so that individuals can simply express themselves, and find acceptance and validation. "It's the most comforting feeling when I hear other people sharing the same kinds of feelings, pain, and hope that I have," said Jennifer, a schoolteacher.

Stages of Recovery

The stages of recovery were described by Herbert Gravitz and Julie Bowden in *Guide to Recovery: A Book for ACOAs* as *survival, emergent awareness, working on core issues, transformations, integration,* and *genesis.*

SURVIVAL

The first stage is survival, because without survival, recovery cannot occur. But my research confirms that adult children of dysfunctional homes survive by approval seeking, acting out of fear, and disregarding their own feelings.

Jennifer, for example, is the survivor of a single-parent home headed by a codependent mother. When she was nine, her father died suddenly, and her mother entered into a depression that only grew deeper as time progressed. Jennifer's personality formed around her need to cheer up and reassure her mother, something neither she nor anyone else could ever manage to accomplish. As an adult, she manifests her dysfunction when the school principal asks her to take additional students into her already overcrowded classroom. She smiles and says cheerfully, "No problem, the more the merrier." But a silent angry voice in her mind screams, "Why don't you give them to the teacher next door, who has far fewer students in her class! Why do I always have to take the extras!"

Jennifer believes that she must do what her principal asks to win his approval; she is terrified by the idea of saying that she considers her class already large enough, and is accustomed to disregarding the pain she feels in such transactions. Jennifer is living her life based on a strategy of survival that she found necessary as a child.

EMERGENT AWARENESS

In this stage, as a recovering person you *identify* yourself as a victim of alcoholism, incest, rigid religious dogmatism, poverty, physical abuse, verbal abuse, abandonment, or some ongoing trauma that resulted in your being abused and neglected as a child. You see yourself as a "codependent person," which author Melody Beattie defines as a person with low self-esteem whose feelings of happiness or misery depend entirely on how the significant others in your life feel about you. This stage includes a growing awareness of the origins of your personality problems, the insidiousness by which compulsive behavior patterns undermine your efforts to be happy, and the obsessive nature of the thoughts that inevitably disturb your peace of mind. This is the stage of *identification and emerging awareness.*

Sue, a 41-year-old nurse and mother who is just beginning her recovery, told me that she is simply becoming more aware of how she was affected by her parents. "I'm learning to acknowledge my feelings to myself," she stated, "but I haven't got to the point where I can express them to other people. In the past it would not even occur to me to be aware of how something affects me, and take a look at it. As I become aware of the feelings that I have disregarded through the years it's been overwhelming sometimes."

Sue's father was a preacher for an extremely strict fundamentalist religion. When he beat her younger brothers she could hear their screams of agony, but the only way she could cope with the pain was to disregard it, telling herself that her father had to do what was right. Decades later, as she recalls her childhood experience, and as the rationalization of her father's behavior loses its credibility, she can be overwhelmed by feelings of pain and anger that were repressed during the traumatic experience itself.

At this time you begin to realize how dysfunctional your childhood was. Anguish and pain are experienced as you tell your story over and over until the intensity is exhausted. Only then, are you ready to move on to examining your own dysfunctional behavior.

WORKING ON CORE ISSUES

Working on core issues is the next stage in the recovery process. This is a period of time devoted to resolving your feelings of guilt, anger, despair, fear, self-recrimination, the repercussions of specific traumatic experiences, and similar issues. The hoped-for result is the evolution of a sense of self-esteem.

Catherine, a physician in her forties, had been in recovery for about a year when I interviewed her. She was focusing on dealing realistically with her feelings of anger. "This has been the biggest struggle for me," she stated. "Recognizing my own anger and beginning to allow myself to express it is not easy." After a year in recovery, she still had trouble expressing her anger, and often took a day before recognizing the feeling. In situations where there is conflict, and other people talk with agitation, Catherine tended to freeze and shut down. It took her a while to process what she was feeling. Ordinarily very articulate, she would begin to stutter in the face of anger. She felt very envious of people who could express themselves in the middle of a confrontation. As she worked on this issue her attitude changed to accepting anger as a normal human feeling, and she learned to express it in ways that were relieving but not harmful.

TRANSFORMATIONS

As core issues are resolved you develop the ability to change your lifelong behavior patterns. These individual changes constitute the stage known as *transformations.*

Catherine, for example, has begun to transform her lifelong inability to feel and express her anger and to assert her rights.

She cited a recent confrontation with her husband as an example of how her behavior has changed at home. He had told her he would be home at a certain time, and she was anticipating going for a walk while he took care of their children. But he arrived two hours later, and she was angry. Ordinarily, she would discount this feeling by telling herself something like "It's no big deal, don't be so sensitive" and pretend that everything was okay. Instead she spoke to her husband about her feeling. "I just want to tell you I was really annoyed," she told him, "because I was expecting you home at a certain time. I had hoped to go out for a walk and you didn't come home!" They had a discussion about it, rather than a heated argument.

This new behavior helps Catherine resolve her anger when it is aroused, rather than ignoring it, letting the resentment build, and eventually overreacting and screaming at her children. It is a change in her usual way of relating to others.

INTEGRATION

The *integration* stage follows transformations. As a recovering person you must integrate the new attitudes and beliefs you are acquiring into a cohesive system that supports your affirming self.

During integration you begin to feel that a new person is emerging. Trusted others notice and validate the newly emerging you. For example, as an individual full of rage you change from dealing with your anger as a daily issue to living as a person who enjoys true serenity. Again, as an individual who struggles daily with self-criticism you become a self-accepting person. The sum of many such changes constitute the integrated individual.

Candy, a person who has been in recovery for several years, expressed such integration in her statement of her sense of self. "Today I can totally own who I am," she said, "and take everything that happened in my childhood as an asset. I am grateful that I grew up in my dysfunctional family because my survival techniques are now working for my benefit. Playing the hero role in the family system was not good for me because I was always trying to win the approval of others. But being the hero now means taking total responsibility for my own life."

Such a strong sense of self-acceptance does not come easily to the adult child of a dysfunctional family. It is the result of years in recovery, and can be achieved only by working through the previous stages.

GENESIS

Genesis is unique in its expression for each individual because it involves the creativity of the newly integrated adult. In genesis you begin to realize your capacity for intimacy, contribute to the development of the community, and experience a growing sense of joyful self-acceptance, shared love, and self-expression. You strive to experience the freedom of realizing the potential you were born to manifest. Pain is experienced as a natural sensation of life rather than as a debilitating drain on your life energy.

Louise Hay, the successful healer and author, certainly personifies a person in the genesis stage of recovery from a traumatic childhood. Her attitude toward the self can be taken as a benchmark of this stage, when she states, "Loving the self, to me, begins with never ever criticizing ourselves for anything."

The Characteristics of Adult Children

Children who survive abusive childhoods do so by learning to cope with the dysfunctional blame and denial of their parents. This learning involves conscious choices to adopt whatever beliefs, attitudes, and behaviors work to reduce the stress they feel. Their personalities develop around a sense of low self-worth, constant vigilance to expect the unexpected, and anxiety about what others are thinking, saying, and doing. These beliefs, attitudes, and behaviors are summarized in the list of characteristics of adult children.

The list that I used in my research is given here. Some of the items on this list were identified as more significant than others by the people I interviewed. These people, most of whom attend various support groups, are adult children of dysfunctional parents. After becoming acquainted with scores of individuals over the first two years of my recovery, I asked a representative sampling to participate in my study. I also advertised for participants in this study, and selected people representative of the various stages of recovery. Some had been involved with the process for only a few weeks, others for many years. Thirty-five people were interviewed. These men and women range in age from 22 to 62, in occupation from handyman to doctor, in education from high school dropouts to Ph.D.'s, and in marital status from solitary single to married with children. They were willing to indicate the characteristics they considered most important in their lives, and to discuss how their beliefs, attitudes, and behaviors changed as a result of their work on these characteristics.

The Characteristics

A. We become isolated and afraid of people and authority figures.

B. We become approval seekers and lose our identity in the process.

C. We are frightened by angry people and any personal criticism.

D. We become alcoholics, marry them, or both, or find another compulsive personality, such as a workaholic, to fill our sick abandonment needs.

E. We live life from the viewpoint of victims and are attracted by that weakness in our love, friendship, and career relationships.

F. We have an overdeveloped sense of responsibility, and it is easier for us to be concerned about others than about ourselves.

G. We get guilt feelings when we stand up for ourselves instead of giving in to others.

H. We become addicted to excitement.

I. We confuse love and pity, and tend to "love" people we can pity and rescue.

J. We have stuffed our feelings from our traumatic childhoods and have lost the ability to feel or express our feelings because they hurt so much.

K. We judge ourselves harshly and have a very low sense of self-esteem.

L. We are dependent personalities, are terrified of abandonment, and will do anything to hold on to a relationship in order not to experience painful abandonment feelings.

M. We have difficulty having fun.

N. We have difficulty with intimate relationships.

O. We lie when it would be just as easy to tell the truth.

P. We have difficulty following a project through to the end.

As experienced by people in daily life, these characteristics fall into four broad categories: the need for approval from others, fear of people, self-alienation, and difficulty with fun and intimacy.

The Need for Approval from Others

The prolonged childhood experience of blame leads to a craving for approval from others. The two characteristics cited by people at every stage of recovery were the tendency to seek approval from others (B), and the overdeveloped sense of responsibility that leads to focusing on the needs of others (F). The tendency to experience guilt feelings when not giving in to others (G) was cited through five of the six stages of recovery. These three characteristics are related to one another to the extent that adult children do their best to take care of others so they can win their approval, and they feel guilty when approval is not granted. The consistency with which these three characteristics were cited highlights the need adult children feel for approval from others.

Fear of People

Underlying the obsessive need for approval from others is a pervasive sense of fear. The three characteristics that express this fear are the tendency to isolate (A), being frightened by anger and any personal criticism (C), and the terror of being abandoned by loved ones (L). At least one or two of these characteristics was also cited by people at each stage of recovery.

The obsessive need for approval from other people and the pervasive fear of those same people combine to create the experience of being victimized (E), another consistently cited characteristic.

Self-Alienation

The most frequently cited characteristics were the tendency of adult children to judge themselves harshly from a sense of virtually no self-esteem (K) and the habit of disregarding their feelings to the extent that they often do not know what their real feelings are (J). In adult children, these two characteristics combine to yield a painful sense of alienation from themselves.

Fun and Intimacy

Finally, the need for approval, fear of people, and sense of self-alienation make it difficult for adult children to have fun

(M), and to relate with intimacy (N). It is not only difficult for adult children to have fun and to experience true intimacy, it is virtually impossible. These are the issues that drive people to seek recovery, and these are the issues that my research identified as most significant.

Other Characteristics

Two characteristics were cited with minimal frequency, and three not at all. The tendency to be addicted to excitement (H) was mentioned by two people who were just beginning their recovery. Surviving the emotional chaos of a dysfunctional home is exciting for a child because the crises that occur stimulate the flow of adrenaline. The constant state of vigilance and high level of anxiety that survivors develop lead to expectations of crises, and anticipation of the resulting excitement. This characteristic seems to be left behind by people as they experience the validation provided by support meetings. Within a few months, as self-alienation begins to heal, the need for excitement lessens appreciably.

Confusing love and pity, and seeking to rescue people (I), was mentioned once by a person who stated she no longer needs to relate to people in this way. This characteristic was not singled out for mention by the people I interviewed because it is very similar to characteristic F, that is, focusing on the needs of others through an overdeveloped sense of responsibility. Many of the incidents related by people as examples of overresponsibility could readily have been identified as rescue behaviors. In practice, these two characteristics are often indistinguishable.

The characteristic of marrying another dysfunctional personality (D) was not mentioned by anyone interviewed. For many people this was too obvious to mention because it is an issue that is usually confronted right away. Jennifer, for example, spoke about her twenty-year marriage to her dysfunctional husband from the point of view of characteristic L, holding on to the relationship because of the fear of experiencing painful abandonment feelings. This was a typical way of viewing such marriage relationships. There is no doubt that this characteristic is common to adult children. The fact that it was not cited is simply due to the preference of those interviewed to look at their own fear of abandonment as the significant issue in their marriages.

Lying when it would be just as easy to tell the truth (O) was not cited by anyone. This is indeed a characteristic of adult children, and some of the incidents described by the people I interviewed could be categorized by this item. Abused children learn quickly that if telling the truth will result in punishment it is smarter to lie. But those survivors who related such incidents preferred to describe them as examples of characteristic B, the need to seek the approval of others. This reveals the motivation behind lying when the truth would be safe to state, namely, the need to say what one believes the other person wants to hear in the hope of gaining that person's approval.

Finally, having difficulty following a project through to the end (P) was not cited by anyone. All of these characteristics do not apply to each and every adult child. This characteristic applies to those adult children who tend to be irresponsible, a trait therapist Sharon Wegscheider-Cruse attributes to the youngest siblings in a family of four or more children. Older siblings tend to be overresponsible (F), a characteristic frequently cited by the people I interviewed.

Spirituality

In the process of recovery you are struggling with lifelong forces that go to the core of your being. The attitudes, beliefs, and patterns of thinking and behaving that you want to change are those that make up your conscious identity. This struggle presents you with the ultimate challenge of life. You cannot endure in this struggle for long without feeling the need to rely on some power other than yourself. Inevitably the question arises: "What resources and power can I call upon to help me succeed in this struggle?"

In listening to the testimonies of scores of individuals, and interviewing the participants in this study, I have found that the concept of a reliable power other than the self is reflective of the individual's stage in recovery. People in the earlier stages either conceptualize a power outside and other than themselves, or are skeptical about any such power. People in the later stages conceptualize a power higher than their conscious selves but within them. They experience it as a force that nurtures and empowers them. In any case the concept of such a power is highly individualistic, and dependent on your background, experience, and emotional and mental needs.

This individualism is respected by the Twelve Step program of spiritual growth advocated by the national Adult Children of Alcoholics movement. Originated by Alcoholics Anonymous in the 1930s, the third step in this program states: "Made a decision to turn our will and our lives over to the care of God as we understood him." Not everyone is comfortable with the word "God," and with referring to God as "him." The term "Higher Power" is often used in group meetings, since it connotes a less religiously defined concept. "It is not important to understand a Higher Power in order to let go," states a very popular book on the Twelve Step program, published by Friends in Recovery. "We need only believe in the process for our own well-being." The emphasis here is to avoid intellectualizing, to encourage you to let go of the need for control, and to trust in the process of growth.

The literature on recovery—indeed, on the meaning of human life—abounds with insights about the spiritual dimension of the human experience. Charles Whitfield, a therapist who is experienced in treating people with alcohol, drug, and family problems, relates the concept of the Higher Power to the Higher Self, or the *true self,* which is within each of us. However we understand the concept, he says, it is the love that resides in our core that is healing.

Scott Peck, a popular psychiatrist and author, believes that the collective unconscious is God, and that the benign and loving realm of the unconscious within each individual is the interface with God. He believes that through the tremendous personal effort required to succeed in the struggle with the conscious self, "We are born that we might become, as a conscious individual, a new life form of God."

Teaching the ancient traditions of the Yogis of India, Yogi Amrit Desai says, "What religions have called the grace of God or the workings of the spirit is actually the working of the life force of prana within us. . . . Prana is the animating force of the entire universe." With a spirituality that respects physical and mental health as the proper channels for spiritual fulfillment and that describes God simply as the natural laws of the universe, Desai's teachings provide guidance for the most comprehensive spiritual lifestyle that I have discovered.

Personally, I believe that whether the concept is expressed as God, the Higher Power, Higher Self, Collective Unconscious, or Prana, the manifestation of this dimension of being in the individual is an irresistible desire to grow in love and acceptance as a form of self-actualizing energy. I believe St. John's statement to the early Christians is one with which all the above cited persons agree: "Brethren, love one another. He who does not love does not know God, for God is love." It is the love experienced and shared in group meetings, therapy, and the development of personal relationships that makes recovery from hostile parenting possible.

The remainder of this book looks at each stage of recovery in more detail, using the testimonies of people who are in the process of recovery to illustrate the dynamics of the stages as they have been experienced in everyday life. It is meant as a guide to the road ahead, so you'll know where you are right now and what to expect in the future.

CHAPTER 2

SURVIVAL

The idea of survival reminds me of adventure stories of individuals struggling against overwhelming odds to remain alive. Such stories are analogous to those of individuals who have survived dysfunctional homes. A small plane crashes in the wilderness, and the pilot is killed. A young woman, her left leg broken, crawls from the wreckage just as it explodes in flames. Such a story then relates how, despite her great pain, she fashions a splint and crutch to enable herself to move, how she finds food, and how she learns to protect herself from the night cold, the hovering vultures, and many other threats. Finally, after thirty days and nights of constant danger, she finds civilization. People help her recover from the disaster handed her by fate, and she is reunited with her loved ones.

Such stories inspire us with their tribute to the indomitable will to survive, and the courage of the individual in struggling against what appear to be insurmountable obstacles. Now, suppose our young heroine has identified the behaviors she learned in the wilderness with her survival. Suppose, for example, she insists on keeping the crude splint she fashioned on her leg, and the crutch that enabled her to hobble through the wilderness, rather than allowing her leg to be treated by doctors. Suppose she reacts to people as she reacted to the vultures that hovered menacingly about her in the wilderness. Her behavior, in society, would be seen as bizarre, and would result in her feeling and being alienated from others. Yet she would feel that she survived by depending on her own wits and energy, and that she could not relax her vigilance by trusting others. If the accident had instilled in her the belief that it happened because she was a bad person, the alienation resulting from her behavior would confirm this belief in her mind. A syndrome would be operating by which this belief would give rise to certain attitudes and expectations, which would manifest themselves as behaviors, and the resulting consequences would confirm the belief. This is the case with you if you have survived a childhood of blame and denial.

In general, in healthy as well as dysfunctional people, the relationship of beliefs, attitudes, behaviors, and consequences can be diagrammed as shown here:

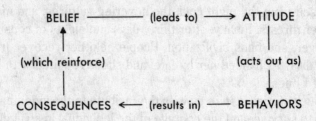

Survival is the stage of recovery in which you find yourself as a result of having grown up in an unhealthy family. It is considered the first stage, just as suffering from cancer is the first stage in recovering from cancer. During survival you are not consciously aware of the core existence of your negative self-belief system. The dysfunctional beliefs, attitudes, and behavior patterns that were modeled for you by your parents have been internalized. They have served as your tactics of survival; you consider them normal.

Tactics of Survival

As a child you were susceptible to accepting negative beliefs about yourself. It is not likely that a rational adult would believe that the plane crash in our analogy happened because that woman was a bad person. But it is likely that a child would believe this if her parent were screaming at her in rage that the accident was her fault. This belief is accepted not only because of the natural bonding between parent and child, but because the child perceives everything with magical thinking.

In the world of magical thinking there are limitless possibilities. Santa Claus knows if you have been good or bad, and will bring nice presents or lumps of coal. Jack Frost paints the leaves in splendid colors every fall. The tooth fairy leaves money under your pillow as you sleep. Your fairy godmother may appear at any time and, with her magic wand, work wonders. Or an old bottle may contain a genie who will grant you any three wishes. More practically speaking, you must be careful not to step on an ant lest it bring rain.

Children love cartoons and Disneyesque movies with fantastic animal characterizations. To remind yourself of this way of perceiving the world you need not take a college course in child development. Simply spend a few minutes watching television on Saturday morning, replete as it is with children's shows. Note how fearful the witches and monsters are, and how magically the innocent protagonists survive the most sadistic brutalities.

In the helpless and unsafe world of the abused child, magical thinking works to create the illusion of power and security. It is natural for a child to accept any belief that seems to work. When confronted with alternatives, the child will choose to believe whatever helps it feel safe. Once a child makes such a choice, however conscious though it may have been at the moment, it begins to operate with a life of its own. Depending on how frequently a negative belief is reinforced by continued blame and denial, it will become a habitual mood state as the child's personality develops.

Unable to grow in self-confidence because of the negative impact of parental abuse and neglect, the child's personality organizes itself around the emotionally dysfunctional syndrome diagrammed here.

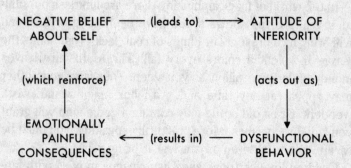

Physical growth will continue through puberty and adolescence. Mental growth continues as much magical thinking is left behind, and the mind becomes more logical. Depending on the individual's talents and ability to use new information, social adaptations and roles develop. Emotional development, however, is limited by the dysfunctional beliefs and attitudes

50

adapted to survive childhood abuse. As a result, the individual suffers from the characteristics of the adult child, listed on pages 39 and 40. These characteristics are associated with a range of negative self-beliefs, typical inferiority attitudes, dysfunctional behaviors, and the emotionally painful consequences they bring until the individual is lost in despair.

Frank

Frank's experience shows how a belief accepted in childhood operates to yield painful consequences as he grows older. Now twenty-three and a full-time undergraduate college student, Frank learned that his father was diagnosed recently as manic-depressive. But what he remembers from his childhood days is coping with a father who was very angry most of the time.

He recalls an occasion when his parents had one of their frequent fights, screaming at each other with his father shoving his mother. Frank took refuge in his bedroom, but his parents entered to confront him. "We're going to get a divorce now," they announced. "Who do you want to go with?" Not knowing what to do, Frank remained expressionless. "You have to pick," his parents insisted. "Come on, pick!"

This was typical of the kind of emotional trauma with which Frank's parents confronted him. As a child depending on his mother and father to help him feel safe, the thought of being abandoned by either of them frightened him. Rather than choose one or the other, he looked at them with a blank expression, and waited to see what they would do. Expressing disgust with Frank's inability to pick one of them, they then left him alone feeling bad about himself.

On another occasion his father yelled at him suddenly,

"Why don't you ever say 'Hi' to me! Do it! Say 'Hi.' " Frank found it difficult to do this, but finally said "Hi." "Other boys say 'Hi' to their dads," his father criticized angrily, "it should be easy for you to do." Although most childhood traumas are forgotten by survivors, Frank now remembers consciously saying to himself at that time, "It would be easy for a good boy to say 'Hi' to his dad. I must be a bad boy."

The choice to believe he was a bad boy was his own conscious conclusion. In a magical way it provided the sense of power and security that children get from hearing the same story over and over. They love also to see movies repeatedly because they feel secure knowing what is going to happen. By believing he was bad, Frank was prepared for the kind of scene he feared, but knew would happen again. On the other hand, if his father's anger was because he was bad, and if he tried hard enough to be good, he might be able to change things. Trying hard to be good meant searching for the magic behavior that would win his father's love once and for all. In either case his belief gave him some sense of control over the situation, and for this reason is considered a survival belief.

Over the years of living with his parents, Frank became skilled at masking his feelings and reactions with an expressionless face. His belief that he was bad led to a fear of people, which prompted him to avoid contact with others as much as possible. During his high-school years, for example, he never went to the cafeteria during lunchtime. He told himself that he was better and smarter than the others, yet he felt ashamed of himself. But his isolation left him without friends, and, as his sexual urges emerged, without the confidence to approach girls. At school dances he felt terrified at the prospect of asking a girl to dance, and being rejected. The consequences were that he was alone most of the time, and his feelings of loneliness confirmed his belief that he was a bad person.

His experience is an example of an adult child survival syndrome:

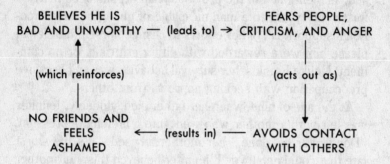

BELIEVES HE IS
BAD AND UNWORTHY — (leads to) → FEARS PEOPLE,
CRITICISM, AND ANGER

(which reinforces)   (acts out as)

NO FRIENDS AND
FEELS ← (results in) — AVOIDS CONTACT
ASHAMED   WITH OTHERS

For Frank, survival meant trying his best to be a good boy. He did his work as diligently as he could out of fear of criticism, and avoided contact with people as much as possible. He walked with his head down, looking at the ground just ahead of him, feeling intimidated by the slightest eye contact with others. He could not relax and have fun, and thought that those who could were pretending. His lack of friends, and feelings of alienation from people, led to a pervasive sense of shame, and confirmed him in his belief that he was bad.

The predominant characteristics that Frank lived by were his isolating himself out of fear, and self-alienation. He was not preoccupied with seeking approval from others because he did not consider that feasible. He felt frustrated and hope-less when it came to having fun or experiencing intimacy.

Jennifer

Jennifer's experience shows how hidden anger can express itself in ways that are self-destructive. She is a schoolteacher and, as mentioned in the previous chapter, has been married for twenty years to a man incapable of giving her any emotional support. All of her efforts to change herself in order to please him were rewarded with either criticism, or no comment. Unlike Frank's, her survival behavior was an obsessive preoccupation with seeking approval from others.

At the age of nine, when her father died suddenly, Jennifer was left with a mother who went into a lifelong depression. "Don't ever be alone," her mother advised, "it's the worst fate that could befall you." Jennifer believed this; her mother certainly provided enough evidence to substantiate the belief. But of greater importance was Jennifer's acceptance of the idea that somehow she had to replace her father in taking care of her mother. Relatives made remarks to this effect at the wake, instilling a sense of guilt in her over her mother's situation. Not allowed to attend the funeral or visit her father's gravesite, her own grieving needs were completely overlooked. Her mother took to her bed and remained in it for two years.

The only love Jennifer received from her mother was conditional, and depended on her mother's mood rather than Jennifer's efforts to please her. If getting A's in school would cheer up her mother, then she worked hard to get all A's. Four A's and a B would be rewarded with the remark that she had to do something about that B. Cruel as this type of comment was, Jennifer's magical thinking set her on the quest for the perfection that would finally please her mother, and win her loving approval.

Occasionally, when Jennifer's mother was in a good mood, she expressed her approval of her daughter's efforts. But these rewards were unpredictable, and impossible to associate with any specific behaviors. Such random reinforcement merely served to confirm Jennifer in her blind search for perfection.

Her underlying belief was that she was not good enough. As in Frank's case, this created the illusion of power and security. If she would just try harder, and do better next time, her mother's approval would be forthcoming. But this belief produced an attitude of guilt, which she acted out by doing her best to comply with the wishes of others. Her approval-seeking behaviors resulted in her being exploited by people, confirming her belief that she was not good enough.

As an adult she acted out this survival syndrome by visiting her mother for dinner every Thursday night, and by staying near her phone every evening in case her mother called and needed help. The dinners were unpleasant since Jennifer's husband and mother used the time together to jointly criticize Jennifer. She responded by trying everything she could to please her husband. He disliked smoke, for example, so she quit smoking. But he never expressed any appreciation for this, or even commented on the change.

At the school where she taught, the principal often asked her to take in additional students as the months went by. As mentioned previously, she pretended to be happy to accommodate him. This was not true, but she craved approval and was afraid of asserting herself with him.

This kind of survival syndrome can continue indefinitely, and become progressively worse, until death, a nervous breakdown, or some other crisis occurs. Jennifer spent twenty years of her adult life attending to the wishes of her mother, trying to please her husband and accepting whatever her boss requested of her. With her own feelings and needs constantly ignored, she sought relief from her pain in overeating and overspending. She used her many credit cards to the maximum limit and eventually found herself with a problem that could not be ignored. Unable to pay her bills, she was also unable to stop her spending.

There is probably no stronger taboo in our society, and certainly in dysfunctional families, than the prohibition against expressing anger toward one's parents. When Jennifer's father died suddenly, abandoning her to the care of a helpless woman, the anger she felt could not safely be acknowledged and expressed in any way. When her mother rebuked her for getting only four A's and a B instead of five A's, her anger had to be stifled. Any show of such emotion would only provoke more condemnation for this "bad feeling." With her husband and the principal of the school in which she taught she continued the same pattern of covering her anger with overpoliteness and consistent cheerfulness. Many adult children develop to perfection the art of being charming in their effort to suppress the forbidden anger burning within their hearts. Another expression of hidden anger is procrastination in the completion of imposed tasks, such as paying credit-card bills.

Forced to parent her mother at an early age, Jennifer's predominant survival syndrome was based on the belief that she was inadequate.

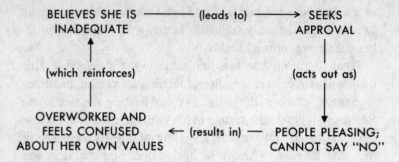

SURVIVAL

BELIEVES SHE IS ———— (leads to) ————→ SEEKS
INADEQUATE   APPROVAL

↑   │
(which reinforces)   (acts out as)
│   ↓

OVERWORKED AND
FEELS CONFUSED   ← (results in) — PEOPLE PLEASING;
ABOUT HER OWN VALUES   CANNOT SAY "NO"

Jennifer's dominant characteristics were her approval-seeking behaviors with her mother and husband, and her fear of people. She was overresponsible in responding to her mother's demands, had lost her own sense of identity in trying to please her husband, and was too frightened of criticism to communicate honestly with her boss.

Sue

Sue's experience shows the effects of what Western psychiatry calls "selective amnesia," i.e., forgetting traumas that are too painful to keep in one's conscious memory. Unlike Frank and Jennifer, Sue was quite sure she did not have any significant personal problems. She grew up in a very religious family, as mentioned in the previous chapter, with her father being acknowledged as the strictest minister of their fundamentalist Christian sect. "Walk the straight and narrow path of salvation," he admonished his children, "and you shall enjoy your reward in the next life, while the sinners of this world burn in hell for all eternity."

Sue did her best to live by this philosophy, and apparently succeeded in building a nice life for herself. Working full time as a nurse, she and her husband lived comfortably with their two teenage sons in a suburban home, with "no more problems than any normal family."

What bothered Sue was her sister-in-law's behavior. Her husband's sister, a charming and intelligent woman, had married a man who beat her. After a typical beating she would call Sue for help, and take refuge in her brother's home for a few days. Battered and bruised, she allowed Sue to take care of her, and listened willingly to her advice. Sue's advice was always the same, "Don't go back to that man." Inevitably, however, after agreeing that this advice was the best course of action to take, the sister-in-law returned to her husband. A few months of peace would follow and another beating would be suffered. From crisis to crisis this behavior repeated itself in a pattern that left Sue feeling frustrated and perplexed. Each time this scenario occurred, Sue grew angrier at her sister-in-law, yet she herself felt there was no other way for her to react to each crisis.

Sue also got upset with people who did not do things right, and on time. For example, her husband and sons had agreed that they would clean their own lunch boxes daily, that this chore was not her responsibility. More often than not they, however, left their sour lunch boxes in the kitchen, claiming they intended to clean them later. Sue could not stand seeing the lunch boxes sitting at the sink, waiting for someone to clean them. She could not refrain from doing the chore, and later arguing with her husband and sons about how and when the job should be done.

In addition, hearing that the hospital where she worked needed help on Saturday nights, she volunteered to be available. Called every Saturday and asked to report to work, she found herself spending every weekend on the job with no leisure time for herself.

All of Sue's energy was directed at satisfying the needs of others. Whether it was her sister-in-law's crises, her family's chores, or her employer's needs, Sue focused her attention and energy on doing what was necessary to keep everything around her running smoothly. Yet far from receiving a sense of personal fulfillment from her dedicated service to the needs of others, she felt frustration over the fact that the other people she served did not seem to appreciate her wisdom, fair-mindedness, and selfless availability. Her assumption was that things would have gotten better if her sister-in-law took her advice, if her husband and sons were more cooperative, and if her coworkers volunteered to do their fair share of work on Saturday nights. But she never figured out a way to control the attitudes and behaviors of the other people in her life.

The desire to control the attitudes and behaviors of others is one of the hallmarks of adult children. Sue tried to get her sister-in-law to change her attitude toward her abusive husband, something his beatings did not manage to accomplish. She wanted to change her husband's and sons' attitudes so that the household would be warm and friendly as they cheerfully took care of their chores. She wanted her employer to approve of her because of her volunteering for extra duty. But she had no magic wand to effect all this, only the vestige of magical thinking encapsulated in her negative self-belief.

The belief underlying her behavior was the more powerful because it was not conscious. What she was conscious of was her attitude that she was willing to help others with their problems, to go so far as to take them on as her own. But the needs of others were like a black hole, draining her energy with no indication that things were getting better. In fact, they got worse, leaving her feeling more and more frustrated. The belief that drove her relentlessly had been instilled by her father throughout her childhood. She was guilty.

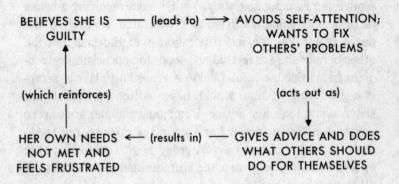

Vital as this belief was to Sue in surviving her childhood, she would scoff at the suggestion that there was something wrong with her belief system. Consciously, she believed that the cause of her unhappiness lay in the guilt of others for being uncooperative and unappreciative. She believed that she would find happiness when her sister-in-law and her husband sought counsel in therapy and learned to change their ways. The last time her sister-in-law sought refuge in her home, Sue insisted that she see a psychotherapist. She went so far as to find a therapist and set up the meeting. When the therapist requested that Sue also attend the sessions, along with her husband and sister-in-law, she wondered why her presence was required. Thinking she certainly did not have any need for psychotherapy but that attending the sessions would help her understand her husband's personality problems, she agreed to attend. As a result, Sue learned that her husband came from an alcoholic family, and that every member of the family had developed personality disorders.

Like many adult children, Sue did not have many specific memories of her childhood. Memories of events that occurred in her home were replaced with vague and general judgments such as "My father was very strict, and my mother somewhat old-fashioned, but that wasn't all that unusual back when I was a child." Focusing her energy on the problems of others helped block recollections of her childhood traumas. It would take several years of therapy and support group meetings to pry open the sealed lid on her memory.

While in survival mode, Sue's dominant adult child characteristic was her overdeveloped sense of responsibility. Focusing on the problems of others left her no time to spend on herself. She would have great difficulty stating what her personal needs were. Her relationships with her husband, sister-in-law, sons, and coworkers were devoid of any true intimacy, i.e., a trustful mutual sharing of personal needs, interests, and desires. This lack of intimacy hurt all the more because she felt she was doing everything right.

Candy

As mentioned in the previous chapter, Candy grew up in a family that denied anything was wrong with the behavior of her alcoholic father and codependent mother. As the reality she perceived was constantly denied, she often wondered if she was crazy. But this was not the kind of belief that could be safely shared with family and friends, so it became more deeply submerged in her subconscious as time passed. Her experience shows how family loyalty and the desire to maintain a good social image can undermine an individual's sense of self.

A capable and attractive young woman, Candy attracted many people of both sexes during her high-school years. With a healthy sense of self-esteem it would have been easy and natural for her to develop many close friendships. But as friendships developed, she found them boring. She compulsively sabotaged them by starting fights, failing to return phone calls, or standing up dates.

Such crises mirrored the conflict in her parents' relationship. It was a painful way to live, but sabotaging her friendships brought about the kind of excitement to which Candy was accustomed. Recreating the crises that she had experienced in her home validated the choice she had made as a child in learning to survive. Since her perceptions of reality had been contradicted by her parents, she felt that other people were privy to some special knowledge about life, and she was deprived of the ability to figure it out. This is the belief that made her feel crazy. Her emotional chaos reassured the wounded child still living within Candy's personality: "You made the right choice," it said, "you really are crazy."

But on the outside, Candy maintained the image that everything was "wonderful." Her family was regarded as successful by her community. A big house, large swimming pool, new cars, contributions to the church, memberships in local business groups and the country club, and the good reputation of the restaurant they owned and operated—all contributed to the image of a happy, healthy family. To talk about alcoholism was taboo within the family. Such talk to outsiders would be regarded as the foulest betrayal.

But behind her mask, the pain resulting from her behavior was experienced as intense self-loathing. Candy's mind would go on for days telling her how incredibly stupid it was for her to stand up that nice boy who wanted to take her to a dance. This inner voice, labeled the "critical parent" by psychiatrist Eric Berne, continued the criticism Candy received from her father. She had been designated by him to succeed him in running the family business. But his way was the only right way to do things. Whether Candy was relating to a customer, hiring an employee, talking to a supplier, using the telephone, or doing virtually anything else, her mind would repeat the reproaches of her father regarding all the things she should have said and done.

What Candy did not understand was that she was not criticizing herself because she had stood up the nice boy, for example. On the contrary, she had stood him up so that she could criticize herself, and thus reinforce the self-belief she had received from her father. This kind of self-criticism never led her to healthy behavioral change, but to the crippling of her will to live.

As she went through her twenties she became progressively alienated from herself.

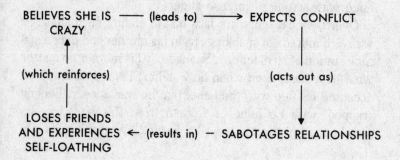

BELIEVES SHE IS —— (leads to) ——→ EXPECTS CONFLICT
    CRAZY

  ↑   ↓

(which reinforces)   (acts out as)

LOSES FRIENDS
AND EXPERIENCES ← (results in) — SABOTAGES RELATIONSHIPS
SELF-LOATHING

The adult child characteristics most dominant in her personality were those of judging herself harshly, and disregarding her feelings. Her sense of self-alienation grew more intolerable with time, and progressed to more self-destructive behaviors.

Jack

Jack's experience shows another survival syndrome common to adult children of dysfunctional families: the need to keep secrets. A Catholic priest in his fifties, his childhood had been spent surviving a sexually and physically abusive mother and raising his younger siblings. He knows virtually nothing about his father even though they lived in the same house till he died in an accident when Jack was seventeen. An immigrant from Italy, Jack's father spent his time at home alone in his workshop, never touching or speaking with his son. His mother's anger was dangerously out of control, leading her to throw Jack from his bassinet when he was only nine months old, breaking his collarbone. At the age of four he was sexually molested when his mother played with his penis and attempted insertion. "Jack, don't you ever tell anyone what we did," she threatened with a tone of intense anger.

Over the next ten years Jack had to endure such abuse as well as hundreds of spankings from his mother and the sexual molestation of an older boy. Spanked by his mother no matter what happened, even when he was hurt in an accident, Jack accepted his fate with the belief that he was a loser. Feeling trapped, with no hope of release from this situation, he sought the love and respect he needed by teaching his siblings to walk, getting them ready for school, and performing the parental role neglected by his father.

After college he entered the seminary and became a priest. His need for approval from others and his workaholic spirit combined to establish his reputation as a devoted, hard-working priest. But nothing in his life provided him with the intense feelings of the punishments and sexual deviations associated with his bonding with his mother. The need of his inner wounded child led him to risky behaviors over which he had no control as an adult.

Erotically inclined toward men, Jack would find himself perusing materials in gay book stores, visiting steam baths, and occasionally picking up hitchhikers for anonymous sex. Throwing caution to the wind he would risk blackmail and AIDS to act out behaviors that resulted in his feeling guilty and "shamefaced." These were the feelings he had grown to interpret as signs of attention from his mother. Needing love from her as completely as any child needs love from the mother, his magical thinking associated his induced guilt with her love.

Unable to express his anger at the annoyances of daily life, the rudenesses of others, and the frustrations inherent in his work, Jack's tension mounted steadily as weeks passed. To relieve this stress, his inner child would take over and play out a series of routines over which he had no control. It was when the stress became unbearable that he would find himself entering a trancelike state of mind, his body moving like a robot controlled by someone else, until his homosexual behaviors were completed. This release from his stress resulted in intense shame, and he would wonder as he drove home, "Why do I do that?"

His wounded inner child could not be stopped by his rational mind from acting out the syndrome associated with his survival of sexual and physical abuse.

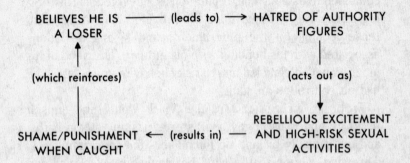

Although his rational adult mind was revolted by his "shamefaced" activities and he took every precaution to avoid being publicly exposed, his inner child wanted to be caught and punished. As Eric Berne explains, this desire is like that expressed by children playing hide-and-seek. It is no fun playing the game if you are never caught. The whole idea of the game is to create a little suspense about how long it will take the other person to find you. But find you he must, or the game itself is defeated. Inevitably, Jack's inner child accomplished this, and won the attention for himself that he craved as the most intensive kind of love he had ever known, namely, the bonding with his punishing mother.

Jack was arrested for illegal homosexual soliciting, and eventually his bishop released the story to the newspapers. When his mother read it she said, "Jack, I always knew there was something rotten inside of you." The survival tactics of his inner child, which Jack experienced as compulsions and obsessions, succeeded in bringing about the consequences that validated the only logical choice he could have made as a survivor of his mother's abuse, namely that the magical way to bring a trauma to an end was to realize that he was a loser.

The survival attitudes and behaviors that characterize Jack are his fear of authority figures and any expression of anger, together with his inability to feel and release his own anger and other feelings. His experience demonstrates the function of denial common to survivors of abuse. The part of himself that was identified with survival seemed ugly and repugnant to him. He never associated his high-risk behaviors with the person he was as a priest. Only when that inner child receives the nurturing love he never got from his mother will he be able to grow beyond his learned survival tactics.

"Adult Child"

The survivors described in this chapter demonstrated certain predominant characteristics in their behavior patterns. Frank isolated himself out of fear of people, Jennifer became an approval seeker, Sue focused on the problems of others, Candy grew increasingly self-alienated, and Jack found himself addicted to risk behaviors. Yet each manifested the other characteristics when their life situations called for them. Frank, for example, was submissive and obedient to his employer as his way of seeking approval. Jennifer overate, and this resulted in the sense of self-alienation that can accompany substantial weight gains. Sue's constantly growing anger led her to isolate emotionally from others by means of her workaholic schedule. Candy often took on jobs for overbearing people in her attempts to win their approval. As a chaplain, Jack tried to please everyone to win their approval.

All felt that they were victimized, found intimacy elusive, and had little, if any, fun in their lives.

Each of these survivors exemplifies one dysfunctional syndrome, showing how given circumstances were reacted to on the basis of a specific negative self-belief. But all adult children have within themselves the beliefs that they are bad or unworthy, inadequate, guilty, crazy, and the guardians of secrets. Although most are not consciously aware of these beliefs, they cope with life using a variety of dysfunctional syndromes as their tactics for survival.

Each syndrome represents a split in the adult child personality, with the number of such fragmentations depending on the extent and nature of the abuse experienced in childhood. These syndromes, based on the beliefs, attitudes, and behaviors needed to survive as a child, have become *ego states* that control you as an adult. An ego state is a temporary identity that you automatically assume to deal effectively with the anger of others, their freedom to abandon, reject, or exploit you, and whatever else you perceive as a threatening situation.

Frank, for example, wanted to dance with pretty girls at his high school, and the rational part of his mind knew that he was an attractive, intelligent, and nice guy. He saw his friends asking girls to dance, and knew how to do it. But every time he made a move toward a girl his survival ego state of *fear* took over and froze him. Jennifer knew she had to pay for things she bought with her credit cards. She knew how much income she made, and how to add up the totals of her expenditures. The adult part of her personality had no problem accepting responsibility for her purchases. But her child ego state of *feeling inadequate* even about expressing her own anger took over when the bills came, and resulted in her procrastinating about payment indefinitely. Sue the adult knew she could call up her hospital and tell the administrator to take her name off the list of Saturday night volunteers, but her survival ego state of *guilt* would not allow this. Candy knew she could avoid her self-loathing by following through with her friends on what she had promised, but found herself "playing games" with them that would bring nothing but trouble. Jack knew that his job and status as a priest depended on complying with the policies of his bishop, but other dynamics were at work in his life over which he had no conscious control.

Within each of these adults was a child who had found safety within the realm of magical negative thinking, and had not been allowed to grow beyond the ego state of the constant wariness needed to survive. Bewildered as adults, they wondered what could be wrong, read self-help books, and repeated their affirmations. But their inner ego states proved too tenacious for self-help techniques. Their child ego states were threatened, and, charged as they were with years of survival energy, they would not change simply because some book offered a rationale for "healthy living." Such efforts to change their syndrome behaviors resulted only in discouragement with themselves, a heightened sense of shame, and a greater need to deny that there was anything wrong.

Many inspirational self-improvement books, such as *Your Erroneous Zones* by Wayne Dyer, offer "bold but simple techniques for taking charge of your unhealthy behavior patterns," and express wonderment at the myriad self-defeating behaviors that so many people manifest. Yet soap operas, novels, and most serious dramas portray people caught endlessly in their own dysfunctional syndromes, doomed to repeat attitudes and behaviors that simply do not work to bring them the love and respect they so desperately seek. Adult child behavior patterns are common knowledge. They abound in the arts, the news, and most of the people who make up our churches, school systems, corporations, political entities, and society as a whole. But what makes it extremely difficult for rational and capable adults to admit their helplessness over their dysfunctional patterns is the secret embarrassment about the magical thinking still operating in their traumatized child ego state. It takes courage to acknowledge that the tactics that seemed to work so magically to survive childhood abuse are powerless to produce satisfactory results in adulthood.

The process by which Frank arrived at the conclusion that he was a bad boy happened for every child victimized by continued abuse and neglect. However, as Sue's story illustrated, most children of dysfunctional families tend, as an automatic survival tactic, to forget specific traumatic events, because they are too painful to recollect. Along with the events themselves, the mental process by which the child consciously chose a negative self-belief is also forgotten. It usually requires personal therapy and support-group work to reawaken one's consciousness of such choices. The purpose of such reawakening is to understand why we made such choices as children, accept that we did what we had to for survival—it was the only form of self-love feasible at the time—and love the inner child who was abused and alienated.

The same belief-expression process worked in the development of self-beliefs for children of healthy, nurturing parents. The difference, of course, is that the self-beliefs adapted by the magical thinking of the child were positive self-affirmations. If this was the case with Wayne Dyer, who states he has always had a sense of inner serenity, and does not

remember where it came from, it would account for his wonderment at the fear and approval seeking he observes in
others.

The self-affirming syndrome has the same dynamic as the
survival syndrome:

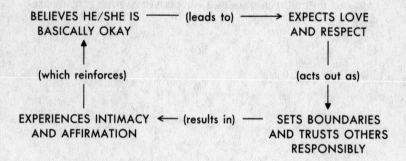

Most people, even those from dysfunctional families, experienced some affirmation as children. What your parents were
incapable of providing may have come from a friendly neigh-
bor, a caring teacher, a loving grandparent or other relative,
or someone else. The affectionate trust shared with a pet may
have been the most affirming experience for some. Thus, in
addition to the negative self-beliefs by which you attempt to
protect yourself from harm, you have positive self-beliefs that
yearn to express themselves in trusting love. The opposite
needs of the protective self and the loving self create the
inner turmoil experienced as emotional pain.

Within the soul of each individual a struggle takes place to
act out those behaviors that reinforce the positive self-beliefs
on one hand, and the negative on the other. Adult children of
dysfunctional families are handicapped in this inner conflict

because of the years of reinforcement they received from the people with whom they most identified and bonded. If you are such an individual, the first step toward tipping the balance of power in favor of your loving self is to acknowledge that you need help, and, mustering all your courage, to ask for it until you find it. Once trustworthy help is found, you can begin to enter the next stage of recovery, emergent awareness.

CHAPTER 3

EMERGENT AWARENESS

If you are the survivor of an abusive childhood, then at some point in your life you may find yourself jolted out of the survival pattern. The passage from survival to conscious recovery is not an intellectual one. It is based on some confrontation with the basic truth that you are in serious pain, and all your efforts to break free of it have failed. They have, in fact, resulted in a no-win crisis, in an emotion-based awakening.

The survival syndrome explained in the previous chapter follows a downward trend of reinforced self-sabotaging as you grow older. The emotionally painful consequences of dysfunctional behaviors grow progressively worse. As negative self-beliefs are constantly reinforced, the attitudes they engender grow more sour and are acted out in ways that are increasingly self-destructive. This process can be visualized as a downward spiral:

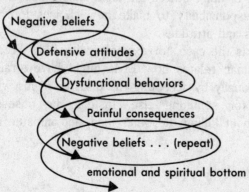

Negative beliefs

Defensive attitudes

Dysfunctional behaviors

Painful consequences

Negative beliefs . . . (repeat)

emotional and spiritual bottom

The "bottom" is an emotionally and spiritually painful experience that convinces you your efforts are futile, that you need help. Of those who find themselves consciously entering recovery some have survived a serious suicide attempt. Others recognize a pattern in their behavior that troubles them, such as forming liaisons with a series of abusive lovers, losing jobs regularly, or even being arrested. Others are seeing a once loving relationship fall hopelessly apart. Usually it is some deep emotional disturbance that cannot be palliated that signals the survivor's bottoming out.

The experience need not be as dramatic as a suicide attempt, lost job, or wrecked relationship. Essentially, it is any experience involving a conscious breakdown in the magical thinking carried over from childhood, and prompting you to seek help to more effectively deal with reality.

When you hit bottom you realize that you have tried everything, and nothing has worked. Despair can creep into your consciousness and move you to accelerate the self-destructive behaviors that seem so essential to your surviving. For many, recovery is never embraced. Despair and self-destruction are the outcome of their obsessive pattern of blaming others for their unhappiness and denying the responsibility to make new choices for healthier self-beliefs and attitudes.

Such was the case, for example, with Elvis Presley. Albert Goldman relates how Elvis might have straightened out emotionally by accepting the disaster of his wife leaving him for someone else. Instead, he obsessed for months about killing the other man, and initiated arrangements for having him murdered. At the moment of decision he backed away from consenting to the deed, but rather than ask for help, he retreated from the truth about himself into a dreamlike state, with round-the-clock intake of drugs. The bottoming-out is a crisis that signals a commitment either to getting well or accelerating self-destruction. For you, hopefully, your suffering has made you strong enough to learn the truth about yourself and the world in which you live.

Frank's case shows a common experience of adult children. At the age of twenty-one, he became alarmed at his inability to concentrate. While reading an assignment for his English literature class, he noticed he had no idea what he had read as he finished a page. He read it again, with the same result. He read it ten times, and still could not get his mind to focus on what he was doing. His mind was so preoccupied with obsessing, and criticizing himself for not being able to understand what he read, that he finally had to quit trying. "There's something wrong with me," he admitted. "I need help."

If this does not seem like a very serious case of bottoming out, remember what an isolator Frank was at that time. His whole hope of making it through life depended on his attitude of doing everything by himself, with no help from others. To him it was catastrophic that he could not focus his mind on reading a simple page of literature.

Because his mother had begun her own recovery by attending support group meetings, Frank asked her for advice. Her direction led him to the ACOA program, and he started attending their meetings. In this way his awareness of the nature of his personality problems began to emerge.

Sometimes a person is confronted with rehabilitation treatment stipulated by an employer, or court of law. Jack's bishop sent him to a treatment facility after his arrest for homosexual soliciting. Jack resented this, a typical reaction in such cases. But in spite of his resentment, the exposure to psychotherapy and support-group meetings engendered a growing awareness of the nature of his personality problems.

Sue's preoccupation with the problems of others helped her avoid recognizing and dealing with her own. Her greatest concern was to learn how to control her husband's behavior, and to that end she studied ACOA literature for years. While reading an article about the types of families that produce the same results as alcoholic ones, she was struck by the phrase "rigid religious beliefs." This led her to wonder about herself. After all, she had decided to marry and have children with an adult child of an alcoholic.

Acknowledging that there might be something amiss in her own personality, she began attending ACOA meetings for her own information. There was much for her to identify with in what she heard, and she began looking at her own behaviors and the painful consequences they produced.

In every case, the focus at this stage is the awareness of problems as a preliminary to understanding where they originate and how they might be dealt with. Viewed in terms of the diagram of the adult child syndrome, this stage brings a growing awareness of the relationship between a person's own dysfunctional behaviors and the painful consequences they produce. This is the first crack in the wall built up by years of blame and denial.

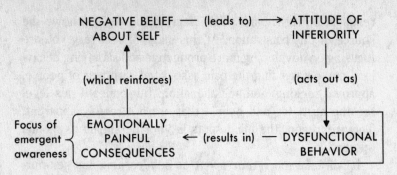

The rewards experienced at this stage include an exhilaration at discovering you are not alone with your fears and problems, a relief at understanding that your personality syndrome is the result of childhood forces over which you had no control, and a great sense of hope that you can finally deal effectively with the debilitating characteristics of adult children. The frustrations experienced at this stage stem from your efforts to eliminate painful consequences by changing your behavior patterns. As you begin to take responsibility for these consequences and understand how they result from your behaviors, you will expect them to change to healthier patterns. But many of your dysfunctional behavior patterns will continue unabated even though you are fully conscious of them while they are occurring. At times you will feel overwhelmed by the challenge of changing so many lifelong habits.

On the one hand, the hope inspired by the experience of emergent awareness will spur you toward a fuller commitment to your own recovery process. On the other, you can expect your frustration at the rate and extent of the changes you can implement to be discouraging, and sometimes to result in outright panic. The diagram (on p. 77) shows the source of this frustration. At this stage of recovery you are focusing on developing more productive and satisfying behaviors, and on avoiding the pain associated with fear of people, approval seeking, and self-alienation. But beneath this level are the attitudes and beliefs that are not readily apparent. They represent the blind spots in your personality's modus operandi.

It will take more time spent on self-learning and self-nurturing to get in touch with your defensive attitudes and negative self-beliefs, to understand how they affect your life, to accept them, to forgive those who engendered them, and to grow beyond them. But while in the stage of emergent awareness you have all you can handle in dealing with the more obvious issues of how your behaviors are wreaking havoc in your life.

The joys and struggles of emergent awareness are shown by those I interviewed who were new to recovery.

Sam

Sam's experience shows that the joys and renewed hope offered by emergent awareness are indeed healing but can lead to unrealistic expectations for a quick fix to one's personality problems. He had begun his recovery from childhood abuse and neglect only six weeks before I interviewed him. He was exhilarated at the changes taking place in his life owing to the insights and feeling of acceptance derived from his support-group meetings. Describing one positive change after another in various aspects of his life, he was enthusiastic about the ease with which his personality problems were being resolved and optimistic about his future.

The director of underwriting for a major insurance company, at forty-two Sam was coping with the divorce of his twenty-year marriage. A friend suggested he attend ACOA meetings to deal with his isolatedness. Sam quickly identified his problems as due to being emotionally orphaned at the age of five when his brother was born with a club foot, and his ailing grandmother moved in to spend her last years with his family. Ten operations were required to mend his brother's foot, and his grandmother died after several years in his home. To compete for attention he became a high achiever at school, earning top grades, and excelling at golf and bowling. Ignored, he worked ever harder, and learned to anticipate everyone else's needs while putting his own on the back burner.

Once Sam knew what the problem was, he felt that the solution was obvious and simple. Believing his life had taken a turn for the better, he was determined never again to make the mistake of neglecting his own needs. He summed up the approval-seeking behaviors that had structured his marriage by stating, "I did not do things for my own enjoyment. Now," he asserted, "I am working to make me feel special."

Citing several rewarding changes in his behaviors, he described how his interest in music had been rejuvenated by singing and guitar lessons, and how he had asserted himself at work by telling his boss what his needs were. Of greatest importance to Sam, his new awareness had enabled him to avoid getting tangled up in sexual liaisons with women who could not be emotionally supportive.

Sam expected that he would be healthy enough to establish a satisfying intimate relationship in the near future. Buoyed up by the successes he had experienced in perceiving needy women as not good for him, he anticipated meeting a healthy woman and finding the love he desired. Yet when he described his experiences of having fun with a woman he had met recently, it was obvious that he did not know what fun is. He seems to have had very little experience with fun as a child. For Sam, childhood had been a time for serious business. Deep inside, he has some anger to get through, anger at a childhood spent competing for good grades and the high bowling and low golf scores needed in his constant effort to win love from parents who did not care about him. He will have to feel the grief over this as he mourns his lost childhood.

You can expect that beneath the joy and relief of emergent awareness are many other feelings you are not yet in touch with. As these feelings gradually emerge they will indicate issues that demand arduous self-parenting. Sam testified to this a year after I first interviewed him. Things had been more difficult than he had anticipated. In spite of this, he said he felt much better and had a more realistic attitude about his recovery process. He had not yet met a woman with whom he wanted to develop a relationship. Instead, this goal had less urgency because he had learned to make friends and develop his own support network.

This early stage of recovery is the beginning of a process that Sam is only partially aware of. The well-run group meetings that he attended encouraged him to accept himself, express his feelings, and get them validated. The old self-beliefs that prevented him from acknowledging and expressing his own feelings were gradually being replaced.

Yet as he delved deeper into his feelings, they constantly brought new issues to his awareness. Music lessons, assertiveness at work, and some clarity about his relationship needs provided a good start on the path of self-actualization. But a good start does not mean the end is in sight. Anger over his lost childhood is one of many serious issues that will inevitably confront Sam as he allows his awareness to grow.

Todd

Todd's experience with the first stage of recovery shows how an adult child's intellectual understanding can exceed his emotional development. This can make growth through the recovery process more painful than actual childhood development. For example, you can understand intellectually what you want in an intimate relationship, but have an agenda of emotional habits that must be unlearned before intimacy is possible.

At the time I interviewed Todd, he had been working his recovery program for six months, attending ACOA meetings regularly, and keeping a journal of his thoughts, feelings, and decisions. For three years he had been meeting with a therapist. Like Sam's, Todd's main concern was developing an intimate relationship with a woman. He attributed his difficulties to parents who fought constantly throughout their lives. He was forty-four, had a Ph.D. in chemistry, worked as a salesman for a high-tech product, and was divorced. His bottoming-out had come when his twelve-year-old daughter insisted he never see her again.

After six months of focusing on his recovery, Todd expressed no exhilaration about the process. Rather, he conveyed the attitude that recovery was an unwelcome but necessary part of his life. He was trying to do what almost everyone seems to try after a few months of emergent awareness, namely, to share his insights with his mother in the hope that she would understand and accept him.

The same day I interviewed Todd, his mother had told him

on the phone that he was "stupid and inconsiderate." His response was to say, "Mother, I feel better about myself and I don't need to listen to that. If that's the way you feel you're entitled to it, but I feel that's inappropriate behavior on your part and I will not listen to it." Todd stated to me that this indicated a strengthening of his self-esteem and his ability to accept his own evaluation of himself over someone else's. His comments were very intellectual, with no indication that he had any feelings of hurt or anger in this incident.

But he also thought that by explaining his feelings to his eighty-three-year-old mother he could get her to understand him. He expected her to begin to modify her abusiveness, but he was disappointed when he visited her at Thanksgiving. She was as adamantly abusive toward him as ever. He then decided not to spend Christmas with her, and planned on having dinner with his ACOA friends instead. He told his mother he would see her the day after Christmas. She was upset about this and, as is typical in dysfunctional families, complained to his sister rather than confront him directly. He then wrote her a letter to clarify his position.

Dear Mom,

    I spoke with my sister last night, and she tells me that you are in a lot of pain and do not understand my not coming up for Christmas. I do not know how to explain it except to say that I love you very much. I do not want to hurt you, but I need, for my own sake, to have Christmas here. I am in a great deal of pain and am dealing with a time of my life during which I am not satisfied with my behavior. I do not want to repeat a lot of this dysfunctional behavior. I need time alone, and with a support group of people dealing with similar problems. I need to sort out what happened to me, what I feel about it, how it affected my behavior, and how I can change my behavior and life attitude. These are all questions no one in the family can help me with. As a matter of fact I have to answer them myself, for myself.

Until I have done this, my pattern of lots of jobs and lots of relationships with women which end badly will be repeated over and over again. I have decided to end this pattern, and, in the course of doing this, need to find out, for and by myself, who I really am (not what I am, for I know that, and so does everyone who can read my resume), and who I really want to be (again, not what I want to be, for everyone wants to be healthy, wealthy, and wise). Once I have found out who I am and want to be, I can begin to pattern my behavior, learning from past mistakes, which I have so far avoided doing very nicely, to live a meaningful and peaceful life, with (hopefully) enough of me to share in an intimate and loving way with family and friends.

All of this may still not make sense to you, but it's the best I can do to explain to you why I need space and time away from family (and, often, even friends) to sort, think, and feel my emotions without input from anyone else.

In this letter Todd expresses no anger toward his mother, and in discussing it with me he would not admit to even the slightest bit of anger. He thought that a loving and logically stated explanation of his needs would win from his mother the acceptance he wanted. But when he visited her after Christmas she was more vituperative than ever, and let him know just how stupid and inconsiderate he was in her eyes. Still, Todd refused to acknowledge any anger toward her.

Instead, his anger poured out at the woman who was his boss at the time I interviewed him. "Inconsiderate" was too tame a word for her. "Stupid, dominant, and crazy" was how he described her, as he assured me he would not be working for her by month's end. Because Todd believed that feeling and expressing any anger toward his mother was incompatible with loving her, he was blocked from feeling a major part of who he really is. His anger at his parents must be acknowledged, that is, felt, and accepted by him as a valid feeling, before he can heal. One of the consequences of this block is that he was still working for the same boss a year later, still traveling extensively for little pay, and still complaining about her.

This letter points out several things that you can expect to experience during this stage. Todd felt hopeful about sharing his newly found awareness about the dysfunctions of codependency with his family of origin. After all, codependency is a family dysfunction, and once he had found the explanation and experienced the treatment for it, he felt obligated to help others still in misery.

If you want to do this I doubt that anything I have to say will stop you. But you need not get your hopes up. If you are experiencing emergent awareness, it is because you are ready for it. It is not likely that others in your family are also ready for it at this time. You are cautioned about this not because your family's recovery is not feasible or important. It is. But your concern at this time is best focused on yourself. Trying to rescue others, or to get them to change, is part of the dysfunction of codependency.

You may feel guilty about getting better while others you care for are still wandering about without direction. How can you feel so good while others close to you remain in pain? Expect to feel such guilt. Let yourself feel it, unpleasant as the experience may be, and talk about it with your support group. They will understand, and you will probably grow stronger in your commitment to your own recovery. This may be something new that you are beginning to realize. You are responsible only for yourself. As with Todd, such guilt feelings will only be resolved by acknowledging your deep-felt anger toward those who abused you. However, at the stage of emergent awareness, you are probably not ready for that. But feel your feelings. They will not harm you.

Are you thinking, as you read this, "If only X were reading this? It's just what he or she needs to know. I will see to it that he or she gets a copy of this book and reads just the section that applies." Let me make a confession here. I have done that. I do not know anybody in recovery who hasn't. There is a name for this type of behavior. It's called code-pendency.

The reason for urging you to be cautious about sharing your awareness with your family of origin is that you can prefer to protect yourself. This is an option made available to you by the recovery process. If your family is dysfunctional then your efforts to enlighten its members can bring about attack and sabotage to your recovery. Your family members are likely to see you as bad, wrong, causing trouble, being selfish and ungrateful, and so on.

Todd's letter expresses his love and concern for his mother as well as his desire to attend to his own needs. Difficult and painful as it is for him, he is letting go of the illusion that his devoted caring for her can make her happy and obtain from her the approval he has sought all his life.

Such letting go is not easy. But this letter serves notice that his priorities have changed. It is really a letter for himself. It is his declaration of independence.

In addition to his letter writing, Todd keeps a journal. This can function as a valuable tool. For example, Todd reviewed his personal notes at the time a relationship with a woman fell apart. He realized that he had disregarded his gut reaction to her from the day they met.

When he gets in touch with the hidden anger toward his parents he can write them letters that will not be mailed, but kept in his journal. In these letters he can let it all hang out, since no one else will read them. This practice is highly recommended at this stage of recovery. Write letters to your mother and father, whether alive or not, and say whatever you feel like saying. But do not mail them. The letters are for your own information.

Other guidelines for journal writing include using a looseleaf notebook so you can add pages as the need arises. You do not have to feel obligated to write every day, but only when you feel the need. Write letters to friends and others that are intended to clarify and express your feelings, rather than to be mailed. Since you are the only person who is to read your journal, you can express yourself without the censorship that takes place automatically in talking and writing to others. This practice will help you get to know yourself and, in times of anxiety, can actually help you relieve stress.

Emergent awareness is a time of transition from a lifestyle based on fear, approval seeking, and self-alienation to one based on parenting yourself. Part of the confusion you will inevitably feel at this stage is due to the limits of intellectualizing. Todd, for example, can discuss his needs with a good intellectual understanding of what an intimate relationship with a woman ought to be. There is nothing wrong with this, and if you are an intellectual person your mind can help you. But it cannot heal you; it has limitations. By masking magical thinking, for example, intellectualizing can block emotional understanding. After stating he would not visit his mother at Christmas Todd wrote, "I do not know how to explain it except to say that I love you very much." Is this true, or is it a magic wand meant to control his mother and elicit a loving response? In fact, it is a bit of both, with his old magical thinking protecting him from the inner fear that if he feels anger toward his mother something dreadful will happen to him.

Emotionally based dysfunctions need emotionally based therapeutic experiences to heal them. When Todd says he has been seeing a therapist for three years and demonstrates no insight about how his repressed anger for his mother is connected to his relationship with his boss, it is evident that his sessions are exercises in intellectualizing. Such "therapy" can continue indefinitely without much healing benefit to the patient.

Sue

Sue's experience shows how the learning that self-discovery brings can be rewarding and frustrating at the same time. The rigidity of her fundamentalist childhood forced her to suppress her feelings. She remembers that if she started to cry for any reason her father would hold his hand before her face and threaten, "Hush right now or I'll give you something to cry about." If she ever expressed anger she was punished with a slap, or by being sent to her room.

After six months of ACOA meetings and two with a therapist, she stated that she was just beginning to acknowledge her feelings to herself. She described this beginning stage of her recovery as an experience in learning. At home with her husband and two teenage sons, for example, she is seeing how she represses her anger until it explodes in rage or sarcasm. She feels grateful to be learning about herself, but frustrated that such behavior is not changing.

The Achilles heel of many adult children is their perfectionism, which holds them in a trap of merciless self-criticism. To counter this tendency Sue expressed the attitude that her growing self-awareness was the most important thing happening in her life. "I'm trying to become aware of how things affect me," she said, "and look at this. In the past it would not even occur to me to do this." She accepted that she could not change her behaviors at that time, and listed things she was learning:

- that it was okay not to be able to correct her dysfunctional behaviors right away;

- to focus on her own needs rather than those of others;

- that there are shades of grey rather than all black or white;

- that her control of others was an illusion;

- that her sense of independence was an illusion because she was so "dependent on others for my sense of self and for approval";

- that it was worthwhile to express her anger in ways other than rage and sarcasm.

Adopting the attitude of a beginner who is keen on learning is the best antidote to perfectionism. Perfectionism is an example of the magical thinking of the abused child who reasons that if she does everything perfectly her parents will have no reason to criticize and punish her. Of course this could never work, but rather leads to the dysfunction described as all-or-nothing thinking.

Sue gives herself credit for the important learning she has experienced in a few months. Her attitude that she is progressing in recovery just by growing in self-awareness and that her behaviors will begin to change when she is ready is worth emulating. Give yourself credit for your own growing awareness, and be gentle with yourself in assessing any behavioral changes.

Jennifer

Guilt was the fundamental motivation that kept Jennifer faithful to weekly dinners with her abusive mother and to her twenty-year-old emotionless marriage. With the help of her ACOA support groups and individual therapy, Jennifer was allowing herself to become increasingly aware of her guilt feelings and how they affected her relationships.

At the time I interviewed her she had been attending three ACOA and Al-Anon meetings a week for five months and had been in therapy for over two years.

Unlike Todd, she expressed passionate anger toward her mother and husband as she described how frustrated she was with them. She articulated clearly the guilt feelings that bound her to them. She was able to speak her thoughts about severing ties with both of them while acknowledging that she felt too guilty at that time to take action and abandon them. Her descriptions of interactions with these key people in her life were well thought out, and charged with an angry determination to make decisions based on what was good for her.

Like others experiencing emergent awareness, Jennifer was not able to change immediately the basic behavior patterns that had structured her life for so many years. But she was able to talk about her problems with a good combination of intellectual thoroughness and passionate feeling. She had to hear herself say the word "divorce" for a while before she would have the courage to take action on one. She had to hear herself talk about letting her mother know she would no longer be at her every beck and call before she confronted her mother.

It was obvious from her attitude of being fed up with abuse and neglect that Jennifer was on the brink of making some major decisions about her life. Over the next few months she went through with her divorce, set boundaries with her mother by seeing her less often, and used her seniority to obtain a more satisfying job at her school. The painfulness of emergent awareness will lead to satisfying decisions, and with each decision a growing sense of self, if you surrender yourself to the process and let it work in its own time.

The Treatment for the Adult Child Syndrome

The treatment that produces healing of the adult child syndrome is participation in support group meetings, and personal therapy. Other important aids to recovery include reading books about the issues, personal-growth workshops and retreats, co-counseling, that is, a structured process of sharing with another, phone calls to supportive individuals, guided-imagery tapes to structure positive meditations, subliminal tapes that suggest a positive self-image to the sub-conscious mind, and physical therapy. Especially if you have been physically abused, I recommend that your psychother-apy be supplemented by regularly scheduled physical ther-apy, such as a Swedish massage administered by a trained and sensitive massage therapist.

Support Group

Participation in support groups allows you to see how others with damaged childhoods are coping with their anxie-ties, approval-seeking behaviors, and patterns of self-aliena-tion. All that is required of you is a desire to get well. The honest sharing of experience, strength, and hope that takes place at meetings provides you with a safe setting to speak of your own fears and difficulties, and with the vocabulary needed to express yourself clearly. When you speak up you feel your own courage, and this nurtures a growing sense of self. Your articulation of what you feel through the ups and downs of your struggle feeds your emerging awareness, and brings validation from the group.

With one exception, all those I interviewed dated the be-ginning of their recovery process to the time they began attending ACOA meetings, although most had been in per-sonal therapy for years prior to that. Saying what they hon-estly felt and thought before a group and finding acceptance was the single most meaningful experience for them. The emotional isolation engendered by their dysfunctional fami-lies of origin began to break down as they found they could reach out for support, and not be criticized for doing so.

Eventually, participation in support groups allows you to develop your own supportive network of contacts. These are people you can call when you are experiencing any problems, even in the midst of a panic attack. You can develop such a network by talking to individuals after meetings, and exchanging phone numbers. Dances, parties, and service activities sponsored by groups provide opportunities for you to broaden your supportive contacts. The atmosphere of support groups allows you to experiment with ways to connect meaningfully with others without the threat of being divorced, fired, or ostracized when you make mistakes.

Sharon Wegscheider-Cruse has stated that her policy as an adult child therapist is to refuse to work with any client who does not have a support network of at least five people. I agree with this policy because the evidence is overwhelming that breaking out of the emotional isolation typical of adult children is essential to recovery. It is as easy for a patient and therapist to isolate emotionally from meaningful connections with others as it is for a codependent married couple.

The one interviewee who did not date his recovery to the time of his first ACOA meeting was Todd. He saw his recovery as starting when he began to read books on codependency. But while the intellectual exploration of his personality problems is a worthwhile exercise, he will make little progress in recovery until he has an emotional breakthrough. Since he has been in therapy for over three years without significantly improving his emotional balance, his sessions are probably limited to intellectual analyses.

Therapy

A good therapist can be as useful to your recovery as a good mechanic when your car needs repair. This comparison is intentional. When your car needs a tune-up or some technical repair work, you value having a knowledgeable and reliable mechanic to do the work. You do not contact the mechanic to become friends, and you do not put him or her on a pedestal as a model human being. Similarly, these are not valid objectives when relating to a psychotherapist.

But since adult children are vulnerable to idealizing their therapists and are not skilled in setting boundaries for interactions with others, it is extremely important to select a therapist who is responsible about these matters. Two helpful practices in this area are getting recommendations for reputable therapists at support meetings, and interviewing.

When interviewing therapists you can ask them what special training they have had with adult child or codependency issues, including their background in child development, and what their attitude is toward your healing. The first question is to determine how knowledgeable the therapist is, and the second, how much he or she cares about clients' well-being. You can ask whether the therapist is an adult child of a dysfunctional family (very many are), and, if so, what treatment she has had for codependency.

After beginning work with a therapist you can periodically evaluate your relationship. Questions to ask yourself are: Is too much time spent on intellectual discussion as compared to expressing emotion? Does the therapist act defensive and like a know-it-all? Does the therapist hide behind big words and evasive answers? Is he uncomfortable with silence? Does he encourage you to participate in support groups? Does he suggest solutions rather than guide you to understanding your problems?

One of the purposes of therapy is to help you discover your blind spots, that is, the negative self-beliefs you chose to survive your childhood of abuse and neglect. Your therapist can give you feedback as you request or need it, can guide your exploration to areas you are blind to, and can facilitate emotion-based exercises such as role-playing and rebirthing. In my therapy, for example, I identified a number of different personalities I can adopt to cope with various perceived threats to my survival. Once such personality is the snarling tough guy. By talking to my therapist in this role I was able to get in touch with that part of myself, understand why I had developed it originally, eventually accept it, and grow to love myself more completely. Rebirthing is a breathing technique that can bring to consciousness experiences you had in the womb and early infancy. It is best practiced under the supervision of a trained therapist.

If your therapist has blind spots they will express themselves by bad judgments regarding the boundaries of psychotherapeutic practice. Elizabeth, an adult child therapist whom I interviewed for this book, described how a blind spot interferred with her practice. Since she had spent much of her childhood trying to prevent her mother from committing suicide, only to have her mother finally end her life by taking poison, she was vulnerable to her clients' threats of suicide. Whenever a client called, even at two A.M., and stated she was going to kill herself, Elizabeth would drive immediately to her home no matter what the distance, and then take her to a hospital for treatment. This behavior is clearly out of bounds for therapy, and is an example of the compulsive rescuing typical of codependents. Only when she had uncovered and resolved her own anxieties over suicide could Elizabeth deal calmly with this issue. She then found that her clients no longer called her to say they felt like killing themselves, implying that such behavior may have been unconsciously suggested by her while her own fear was operational.

Conclusion

The purpose of group participation and psychotherapy is to help you understand the specific choices you made as a child to adopt negative beliefs about yourself. Once you understand why your wounded inner child made such choices, accept them as the most sensible choices you could have made at the time, and love your inner child for doing what he or she had to do to survive, you will be actively healing old wounds. One sign of such healing is making conscious positive choices.

All those I interviewed who were at the stage of emergent awareness were focused on the relationship between their behaviors and consequences. The ingrained self-beliefs and attitudes responsible for their behaviors remained hidden.

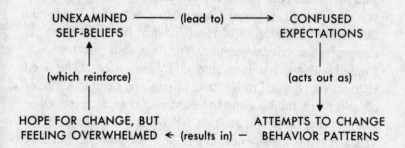

Consciously identifying yourself as an adult child of a dysfunctional family is the first step in the process of healing.

This decision starts the process of conscious recovery. It represents a realistic belief statement that creates new attitudes, behaviors, and consequences.

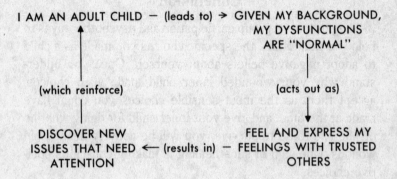

As feelings are encouraged to emerge into the open they begin to show their value as truly vital sources of information about you and your world. Like Sam, you can begin to investigate just what your needs are for intimacy and which needs you can realistically expect others to meet. Like Todd, you can make a declaration of independence from the expectations of your critical parents. You may find yourself confronted with the issues mentioned by Sue, such as the need to focus on yourself rather than others, the need to let go of all-or-nothing thinking and the illusion of control, the need to change your approval-seeking behaviors, and the need to validate and express your anger. And like Jennifer you may feel the need to resolve your sense of guilt. These are some of the core issues that will lead you into the next stage of your recovery.

CHAPTER 4

WORKING ON CORE ISSUES

If you allow yourself to feel your feelings without the censorship that was a necessary survival tactic, you will become more and more aware of how your behaviors are dysfunctional, and how they bring about the very consequences you most fear. As the days go by, this perceived dysfunctionality becomes increasingly intolerable, moving you to take action on certain basic issues. These issues are nothing less than the attitudes that seemed so indispensable to your survival and are so strong within your personality that they take over and determine your modus operandi as fully operative states of mind.

You may want to increase your vigilance over your inner thoughts and feelings as well as your outer expressions and behaviors. You may want to take control of your recovery, put it on a productive schedule, and, as a result, exercise control over your life. Is not this the purpose of recovery, to exercise better control over everything in your life? Actually, the attitude that you have to be in control every minute is itself a survival tactic. This is the most basic of the core issues on which you have to work.

The Obsessive Need for Control

The attitude that you have to be in control stems from your belief as a child that you were in danger, a belief that was not unwarranted. When Jack was thrown from his bassinet at the age of nine months, breaking his collarbone, he learned at that tender age that his mother was dangerous. Parental practices of blame and denial are dangerous to children, and not all survive. Lisa Steinberg, whose father was convicted of beating her to death, could not, at the age of six, protect herself from his violence. To this day her father, Joel Steinberg, denies that he ever treated her in any but a loving way and blames his imprisonment on a general conspiracy. Everyone who attempted to communicate with Joel Steinberg found his narcissistic obsession with control an impenetrable barrier. Extreme cases of the adult child syndrome, such as Joel Steinberg's, are irredeemably narcissistic, and extremely dangerous. Even though your parents may not have been as dangerously narcissistic as Steinberg, their belief system of blame and denial was perceived by you as dangerous.

Those who survive abusive parents know what it feels like to be truly helpless and hurting, to turn for comfort to those meant to protect them, and to then be stomped on with mean rage. The magical thinking of childhood is children's last recourse for safety, as it creates the illusion that they must exercise control over their parents by repressing unacceptable feelings, seeking approval, isolating to hide from them, and manipulating them. Such behaviors only feed into the negative energy of chronic anxiety that confirms the belief you are in danger.

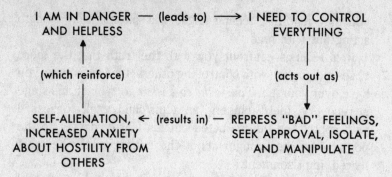

I AM IN DANGER — (leads to) ⟶ I NEED TO CONTROL
AND HELPLESS   EVERYTHING

↑ |

(which reinforce)   (acts out as)

| ↓

SELF-ALIENATION, ← (results in) — REPRESS "BAD" FEELINGS,
INCREASED ANXIETY   SEEK APPROVAL, ISOLATE,
ABOUT HOSTILITY FROM   AND MANIPULATE
OTHERS

As a survivor, your whole focus for years has been on trying to perfect the means of controlling others. One tactic essential to this effort has been the repression of your feelings in favor of mental rationalizations. During the months of your emergent awareness you were encouraged to feel all your feelings. This seemed like an innocent enough exercise at the time. But feelings set off alarms for adult children. If I sense anger, for example, and allow the feeling to emerge, won't it get out of control and hurt or kill someone? Joel Steinberg, who beat his lover for years before killing his daughter, never expressed anger during his three-month trial, which he claimed was nothing but lies. When his frustrated lawyer asked why he did not show anger, Steinberg stated, "I don't like to show anger." In fact, his inability to feel his feelings, and his obsessive denial of having any "bad" feelings, resulted in his acting out his repressed anger as rage. This is a danger to which you are likely to be very sensitive. You have lived with and survived rage, expressed either as physical abuse, verbal abuse, or the silent treatment of passive aggressiveness. In any case you may fear that feeling anger will automatically lead to acting out with rage.

Real feelings confront you with the truth that the more obsessed you are with controlling others, the less control you have over yourself. This is *the core issue* for you at this stage in recovery. Joel Steinberg, an adult child totally obsessed with controlling others, acted out his fear of danger to the point where he brought about the consequences he most feared, imprisonment.

To that part of you that developed the obsessive need for control, often referred to as the "wounded inner child," the need for control is not an illusion but a life-and-death matter. Your wounded inner child will not give up its hold on the need for absolute control without a battle. For your wounded inner child this is nothing less than a struggle to the death. You will need all the support you can get and all the tools you have learned about thus far to face the paradox that the only way to gain control of your life is by letting go of the obsessive need to be in control at all times.

The Twelve Step Program

It is at this point that many people drop out of recovery. They stop attending meetings, and terminate therapy. Others plunge ahead courageously, determined to get to know the wounded inner child hiding behind the obsessive need for control, and to befriend him or her. Many find it helpful, at this stage, to use the Twelve Step program adapted from the Alcoholics Anonymous movement. This program is designed to facilitate letting go of the obsessive need for control. It helps answer the question "If I am going to yield control of my life, to whom or what will it be?" The Twelve Steps give a structured approach to the growth process, as adult children yield control of their lives to their "Higher Power" and talk about "working the program."

The Twelve Step program provides guidelines to the spiritual process of discovering what Yogi Amrit Desai defines as "the basic purpose for which we exist," that is, "an inborn urge to reach to the ultimate degree of internal fulfillment." As a set of spiritual guidelines, the Twelve Steps can provide a meaningful structure to your struggle with the issue of control. You may find such a structure reassuring as you face the frightening prospect of letting go.

Since the Twelve Steps are guidelines to the process of giving up the obsessive need for control, your experience of them is bound to be unique. What I present here is my personal description of the Twelve Steps as I experienced them while struggling to let go. These are adapted with permission of the A.A. World Service, Inc. (For the complete unaltered version of the Twelve Steps of A.A., see the Appendix.)

STEP 1. We admitted that we were powerless over our past, that our lives had become unmanageable.

I realized that my obsessions were out of control, that my anxieties and tensions were making my life unbearable, and that if I did not get professional help I would do something so desperate that my life as I hoped to live it would be destroyed. I acknowledged that my mental and emotional problems were very serious, and that my life was getting worse despite all my efforts at self-improvement.

STEP 2. Came to believe that a power greater than ourselves could restore us to sanity.

I experienced the healing process that the ACOA group support program can provide. I felt hope. I was inspired by the courage of people in the recovery program, and I began to learn about the syndrome that had been making my life unbearable. My belief in my Higher Self was rekindled.

STEP 3. Made a decision to turn our will and our lives over to the care of God as we understood Him.

I committed myself to my recovery by attending ACOA meetings regularly and sharing my thoughts and, after several months of trying, my feelings. I read books about codependency, the inner child, the dysfunctional family system, etc. I made my mental, emotional and spiritual recovery the top priority in my life. I surrendered my life to whatever direction the healing power in my recovery would take.

STEP 4. Made a searching and fearless moral inventory of ourselves.

I focused on myself, and examined the behavior patterns that sabotaged my life. I became aware of the voices of criticism within me that were so discouraging, the "old tapes" and the self-defeating attitudes that underlay my behaviors. With the help of therapy I began to understand how my childhood conditioning affected my adult attitudes, beliefs, and behaviors.

STEP 5. Admitted to God, to ourselves, and to another human being the exact nature of our wrongs.

I recounted in accurate detail how my life had been ruled by obsessive behaviors. I no longer used denial to put frosting over everything. I was honest with myself, my support groups, and individuals whom I trusted, and shared unvarnished accounts of my life experience. Through support-group participation and personal therapy I went after the truth with a vengeance.

STEP 6. Were entirely ready to have God remove all these defects of character.

I realized how self-defeating some of the attitudes and behaviors were that I clung to. I became disposed to let go of them. I was ready to let my Higher Self, the healing power in my recovery, remove them.

STEP 7. Humbly asked Him to remove our shortcomings.

I reflected on my need to change in a spirit of desire for healthy growth. I patiently accepted myself as I was, and expressed my desire for the healing process to remove the old self-sabotaging patterns one by one.

STEP 8. Made a list of all persons we had harmed, and became willing to make amends to them all.

I listened to my conscience without the excuses provided by denial. I identified those persons whom I knew I had wronged.

STEP 9. Made direct amends to such people whenever possible, except when to do so would injure them or others.

I contacted people I had wronged. I made amends and whatever restitution was appropriate in each case. I felt my self-esteem renewing.

STEP 10. Continued to take personal inventory, and when we were wrong promptly admitted it.

When I experience a conflict with someone I contact that person as soon as I can to try to resolve it, and prevent my old obsessive patterns of resentment from taking hold. I take responsibility for my behavior, and let the other person answer for his or hers.

STEP 11. Sought through prayer and meditation to improve our conscious contact with God as we understood him, pray-

*ing only for knowledge of His will for us, and the power
to carry that out.*

By reflecting on my healing process, and expressing my
sincere desire to get better, I am learning to let go of my
obsessive need for control and to allow the healing process
of recovery to take me where it will, as it creates new paths
for the journey of my life. Through daily meditation I experience a renewing contact with my Higher Self.

*STEP 12. Having had a spiritual awakening as a result of these
steps, we tried to carry this message, and to practice these
principles in all our affairs.*

Having experienced the healing and hope of the ACOA
recovery program and of personal therapy, I continue to
participate in it. I am no longer the person who used to
demand that others fill up the vast emptiness I always felt
inside. Instead I live with the peace of mind, courage, and
wisdom that I have learned and continue to learn in the
recovery program and that I can share with others in my life.
With trusted others I have formed a family of choice to replace my family of origin. I feel safe with them and know how
to be a safe person for others who need to trust me.

Control and the Adult Child Characteristics

The obsession with control manifests itself through the
attitudes already identified as characteristic of adult children,
such as the following:

- the need for approval from others, with its tendency
  to turn into overresponsibility and guilt feelings;

- fear of people, with its unrelenting hypervigilance;
- self-alienation, based on a dissociation of present feelings from past emotional traumas;
- difficulties with fun and intimacy, since distrust of yourself and others is so ingrained.

At this stage of recovery you can expect to find that hard work is demanded of you if you are committed to changing your life. You will have to examine how your attitudes are affecting your behavior, and what new attitudes are developing out of your feelings.

The focus at this stage is on the extent to which your behaviors are evidence of your attitudes and, conversely, how new attitudes are affecting your behaviors.

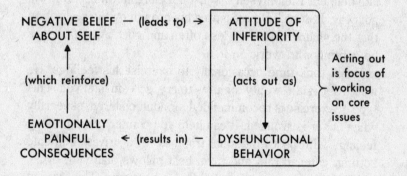

Frank

Frank's recovery shows how feeling his feelings led to a better understanding of and control over his anger. It was his deep sense of shame that kept him isolated all his life, and completely inadequate in relating to people. He walked looking down, with his head bent, feeling unworthy to look others in the eye. Shame would overtake him during a conversation, telling him he was not good enough to be talking to the other person.

As long as Frank did not allow himself to feel the shame in all its intensity, it would take over as a mind-set and direct his behavior with a will of its own. As he began to sit with it, to feel it, to let the sensations of shame run through his body and mind, he found that they did not kill him. His attitude toward his shame gradually changed from perceiving it as who he was to perceiving it as "only a feeling."

A change like this is significant and it may be months before it feels comfortable. Frank described the work he did with his shame. "When it comes up now," he said, "I feel it hurting like hell, but I tell myself it's just a feeling, not me, and it will go away. It does." He measures his growth by the realization that the shame comes up less often and goes away faster as he continues to work on it.

Frank took time occasionally to exercise his feelings. He would set aside twenty minutes to cry, scream, and yell. This type of exercise is recommended for adult children, especially when anger is aroused. It can help you connect your present feelings with past emotional traumas. In a private and safe setting, you can rant and rave, beat pillows, flail your arms, and kick your legs out in a full-fledged tantrum. This type of exercise generally ends with a sense of relief, allows you to get in touch with your feelings, and prevents harm to yourself or others. Venting your anger in this way can build up your ability to read your feelings, just as exercising the body tones up the muscles.

If you notice yourself getting disproportionately angry about something, a tantrum exercise can help you acknowledge anger that stems from unresolved childhood experiences. Suppose you are to meet someone and the person is five minutes late. You feel upset to the point where you visualize screaming at the person, insulting him or her, or even just making a sarcastic remark. Your anger is out of proportion to the event stimulating it. If it is feasible, if for example you are waiting in a car by yourself, you could scream out your rage uninhibitedly. While doing this you would be releasing pent-up anger, and you could have a flashback memory of someone or some event that is responsible for the pent-up emotion.

Frank's old attitude that he is not worthy of others has been replaced with a determination to assert himself. For months he had to force himself to be with people. He consciously observed the consequences. No one, he said, wanted to hit him in the face or say nasty things to him, as his wounded inner child had expected. He gradually became relaxed with people to the point where he enjoyed mingling.

Working on his fear of people involves doing things he has avoided throughout his life. Frank said he "forced himself" to attend dances, ask women to dance, and dance. He noticed his attitude shifting from, "They'll all know I'm a fake" to "Hey, this is really fun! I don't care what people think." But this was hard work for him. Until he was relaxed enough to enjoy going to dances, he had to make the effort. But as he worked on this issue he found that it got easier for him to relax, enjoy group activities, and have fun.

On his summer job he was able to assert himself calmly when his boss lost control of his anger and threatened him. This was a significant difference from his former subservient pattern with this man. He understood that his boss, an independent landscape contractor, was under stress as a result of expanding his business, and had been reacting to people with more anger than Frank had noticed over several prior summers. But that understanding did not block Frank from standing up for himself.

As Frank remembers the incident, his boss gave him a look like he wanted to kill him as Frank returned from lunch one day.

"What's wrong?" Frank said, looking him in the eye.

"Didn't you hear me call for you when you left for lunch?" his boss challenged.

"I thought I heard something, but I looked back and there wasn't anybody around. The others in the truck didn't see anybody so we continued on to get lunch."

"Well, didn't you hear me?"

"No."

"Yes you did, you heard me."

"No, I didn't hear you."

"You had to hear me! Don't fucking lie to me! You had to hear me!"

"No, I didn't hear you."

"How would you like it if I left you here?" he screamed.

Frank said nothing to that since his boss was out of control, and he felt himself starting to get angry at him. He felt under control, and wanted to keep it that way. Instead of getting into a shouting match, he felt his anger, remained calm, and simply looked his boss in the eye. Finally his boss calmed down.

Frank's experience shows that as he became more aware of how his own control mechanisms work he could see more clearly how other people tried to control him. You can expect to experience this as you work on your control issues and, as a result, become more competent in dealing with others. His boss's anger was an effort to control Frank. By shouting and using abusive language, his boss tried to intimidate him. When someone talks to you this way, his or her credibility depends completely on your own sense of shame. Of course, if the person is much bigger than you, and threatens bodily harm, you may have to resort to survival tactics temporarily. That was the case in childhood, but not in instances like those experienced by Frank.

In cases where your financial security is threatened you may decide to resort to survival tactics to give yourself time. In this case Frank's boss needed him more than Frank needed the job. Frank waited a few days to see how things would go between them, got his paycheck, and quit the job. "Sure, he was under a lot of pressure and lost control," Frank stated, "but he should have apologized afterward. That's his problem, not mine."

The normal adult child attitude for Frank in this case would have been to justify his boss's abuse by understanding that his boss was under stress. "He did the best he could under the circumstances" is what adult children say. This reflects the old attitude of taking responsibility for your dysfunctional parents: "They did the best they could." You had to adopt this attitude to survive, because as much as your parents' behaviors angered you, you could do nothing about them. Like Frank, you are no longer so helpless.

Frank put the focus on himself and was able to see that he was not responsible for his boss's anger. In fact, he was quite clear about the fact that he did not deserve such abuse and took steps to avoid a repetition of the experience. Since this was a summer job and Frank lived with his parents, he opted to quit the job and find another. Frank's account of this transaction with his boss illustrates that as he worked on his own shame and anger he could see more clearly how dysfunctional attitudes work in others. Rather than deny his boss's dysfunctional behavior or blame his boss by labeling him in a retaliatory way, Frank simply accepted him as he was and took steps to protect himself from a repeat of the abuse.

Again, this was hard work for Frank. He had to consciously refrain from reacting to his boss's anger with his customary sense of shame, accepting the blame for the other man's being upset, and acting in a way to placate him. Next, he had to consciously take note of how he was feeling while responding to his boss's challenging questions, then his insulting attack, and finally his threat to abandon Frank at the site. As he felt his anger he had to consciously interpret its message and decide what action to take. Frank was not concerned with controlling his boss, but with controlling himself.

Sally

Sally's work on her control issues shows how it has realigned her relationships with her husband, her children, and her coworkers. It shows also how the cycle of passing family dysfunctions from generation to generation can be broken. Her own mother's mental illness was diagnosed as acute chronic depression, and her father was a workaholic who never showed emotion. Sally grew up as a superresponsible overachieving "good girl" and, as an adult child, dedicated herself to pleasing her husband, doing everything for her three children, aged five, seven, and ten, and being frantically busy on her job as a corporate lawyer.

She experienced her bottom five years ago when, at the age of thirty-six, she had her third baby, her family moved into a new home needing extensive repairs, and she tried to rescue her mother from going crazy after her father left her for another woman. Describing herself as her last priority, she remembered when she used to suffer chronic insomnia, eat poorly, blame everyone around her, and feel doomed by the inner voice of harsh self-criticism. She now participates in a Saturday morning ACOA meeting, a lunchtime Al-Anon meeting, personal therapy, marriage counseling, and co-counseling, and takes Fridays off from work to visit a yoga center for rest and renewal.

Sally's obsessive need for control manifested itself in her taking on responsibility for others and neglecting her own needs. In her relationship with her husband, Jim, she pretended to be agreeable after he threatened her with abandonment if she spent too much time with her ailing mother. Furious inside with him and with her father, she put on a cheerful mask for several years. She stated that her recovery work began a year and a half ago, and that she was working hard on taking care of her own needs and asserting herself.

When Jim kicked their seven-year-old in the groin recently, in Sally's presence, her initial reaction was to dismiss the incident by repressing her feelings of revulsion. "It's not that serious," she thought, "this kind of thing only happens once every three months or so." If she accepted this rationalization, then she would not have to challenge Jim's behavior. But her new awareness of her feelings cast doubt on the validity of the rationalization. The crux of the control issue for Sally was getting her gut reaction to her husband's behavior validated, and relying on it as her ultimate authority.

She mustered all her courage and utilized the many tools of her recovery program to confront him. This was very difficult for her because Jim has had ten years of practice at what she calls "shaming" her, that is, arguing forcefully that she is to blame for the anger and tensions in the household. Confronting him in the past would have meant a fight that she would lose by admitting in the end that she was indeed somehow responsible for his kicking their child.

Her first task was to get validation from trusted others that her perception of what happened and her judgment that it was wrong were correct. She discussed the incident with her marriage counselor, who confirmed that Jim's action was indeed physical abuse. The counselor told her that Jim should be warned that if he did anything like that again he would have to leave the house immediately. Sally thought about this recommendation, and confessed that she did not have the confidence to tell him that. The counselor, who meets with Jim also, said he would tell Jim of this policy decision.

Sally then related the whole incident and her discussion with the counselor at her next ACOA meeting. Again, her perception and judgment were validated by other people. By talking of the incident and her feelings about it, she was taking manageable risks that helped her make up her mind about what she needed to do. Such talking was difficult for her. It required that she break the tradition of dysfunctional homes: "Don't feel, don't trust, don't talk." But her counselor and support group provided her with low-risk environments for her to break this tradition. Even if she was "wrong" in speaking as she did, the consequences would not include the abandonment she feared from her husband. After articulating her feelings to her counselor and support group and seeing how good it felt to have her gut reaction validated, she realized she needed to confront Jim herself.

When she spoke to him about the incident he made some

witty remark and tried to laugh it off. Sally told him he was using humor to cover the fact that he was mean.

"The next time you hit one of our kids," she said, "I will tell you to get out of the house."

Jim attempted to blame her. After all, this tactic had worked for over ten years in their marriage. But the validation she had received from others and her determination to stick to what she felt was the truth kept her centered, and she responded:

"You don't want to deal with the fact that your father hit you a lot as a kid and look into the feelings you have about your father. But whether you want to or not, it's affecting our kids, and I will protect them, no matter what."

When Jim insisted Sally was making a mountain out of a molehill, she referred to the validation she had received from their counselor and her support group. He became furious at this, accusing her of disloyalty. "Nothing's confidential," he shouted, "you can't trust anyone!" As with Frank's boss, this is an attempt to use rage to intimidate and thus control her.

"That's how you see it," Sally replied calmly. "That is not true for me. What are you feeling?" she challenged him. "It's shame isn't it, because it was your action that you are ashamed of. I give it back to you because it's not mine."

Hearing her own voice, and seeing herself standing up to her husband by setting boundaries on what were his and her responsibilities gave Sally a sense of self-control she had never been able to achieve by means of her overresponsible pattern. In the past, when she accepted responsibility for Jim's abusive behaviors, no clear boundaries could be established and she would be lost in a sea of confusion.

Her story shows clearly why this stage of recovery is called "working on core issues." She is not yet at the point where she knows confidently what her eyes are seeing, what her feelings are telling her, and what boundaries make sense. Acknowledging this, she makes use of the help others can provide to sort through her perceptions, feelings, and judgments, to determine what tactics are reasonable for the situation, and to assert her rights. Her tools included phrases that she had learned and practiced in co-counseling or read about in recovery books, such as "That's not true for me" and "I give it back to you because it's not mine." Doing all this took time, energy, and a reorganizing of her priorities. It is work.

Sally's real adversary in this confrontation was her self-doubt, not Jim. Any attempt to control him by manipulation would simply entrap her in her own wounded inner child's magical thinking. But she was determined to act as an adult with responsibilities to protect herself and her children from the adult child syndrome that made her own childhood so dysfunctional.

This example of Sally's recovery makes clear that she was not trying to improve her marriage by manipulating her husband. She first took the responsibility to improve her relationship with herself, and as a result found herself in a position to help her husband change. She first learned to let go of her obsessive need to control him by the approval-seeking behaviors learned in childhood. As she came to see more clearly what her responsibility in their marriage was and was not, she could help him see his. In this example, she told him he was responsible for dealing with his own issues, stemming from his childhood experience of physical abuse, and made it clear what consequences he could expect if he refused to do so. She was not threatening him, but trusting in herself and in his willingness to act responsibly.

Jim had a responsibility to look at how his experience of physical abuse as a child affected his behavior toward his own children. This is one of the issues on which he has to work if he is determined to act as a responsible parent. The attitude expressed by many adult children that the past is over and done with and that talking about it is engaging in self-pity is simply an expression of their denial. Working on recovery means discovering what attitudes underlie dysfunctional behaviors and taking responsibility for them. This itself is an attitude that replaces the pattern of blame and denial. Since Sally had been doing this for herself, she was in a position to help Jim pursue this process.

During the previous ten years of their marriage Sally was stuck in her own pattern of obsessive control and could not help her spouse face the consequences of his behaviors. By accepting the rationalization that his hitting the children was understandable because it happened at three-month intervals, she was *enabling* her spouse's abuse. Enabling is supporting another person in his or her dysfunction by denying responsibility for the consequences. It is often called being "understanding," "forgiving," or "loving," since denial necessarily expresses itself in euphemistic terms. In fact, however, the enabler is acting as an accomplice. Both spouses are responsible for the abuse since they are enmeshed in the same syndrome.

This codependent enabling syndrome can be diagrammed as shown here, with the understanding that both parents collaborate in the syndrome.

115

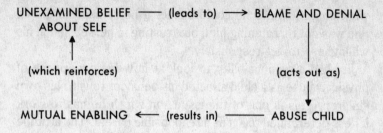

Having begun the process of examining her attitudes, Sally was in a position to break this cycle in herself and to help Jim see how he also could break it. In any case, she no longer supported his neglecting to examine his own attitudes.

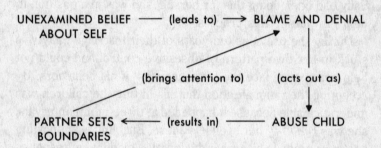

This diagram shows how the partner's role shifted from reinforcing the negative self-belief to focusing attention on the attitude expressed by the other partner. When you have done this for yourself, you are in a position to help your partner, if you have one. In any case, however, the negative self-beliefs that underlie your attitudes of blame and denial may remain unexamined for a time as you work on the core issue of control. For the present, it is demanding enough to unravel the ways in which your attitudes are acted out as dysfunctional behaviors. No sooner do you come to understand how one attitude expresses itself than another crops up to grab your attention. Each new attitude problem is, of course, generated by the unexamined belief about yourself of which you are unaware. You may get discouraged as it seems that life is presenting you with an unending succession of issues on which to work.

But any negative self-belief you have conflicts with your inner urge to self-fulfillment and generates the attitudes and behaviors that result in pain. This pain has a natural function in your life. It acts like a beacon guiding you on to discovering deep within yourself that negative self-identify that you developed as a wounded child. Eventually it will dawn on you—and I repeat, this is an emotional rather than an intellectual experience—that this wounded inner child, ugly and repulsive as she may appear to you with her deformities, needs your gentleness, your loving care, and your warm embrace to begin to heal. When you reach out to yourself this way, embracing your inner child with all the love and attention you have been lavishing on others, you will experience the healing power of your own love. This is the "miracle" many people in recovery refer to when talking about their healing experience.

Sally still finds it necessary to criticize herself. At the end of our interview she made the comment, "I talk this better than I do it." She does not really need this perfectionism. Perfectionistic self-criticism merely keeps the wounded inner child in hiding and its negative self-beliefs operative. The single most difficult concept for you as an adult child to absorb is the belief that it is okay to accept and love yourself, just as you are, right now.

By improving her relationship with herself, Sally has also

117

changed her relationship with her children. She used to pamper them, doing things they should learn to do for themselves such as preparing breakfast and getting the children dressed for school. This changed when she decided she needed to begin each day with a yoga meditation exercise to calm her mind and a run to awaken her body. As she began to focus on her own needs and change her habits, the old patterns disappeared. At first, the children reacted like Jim in the example above, attempting to make her feel guilty for neglecting them. She let them know they were old enough to prepare themselves for going to school. Gradually, a new pattern emerged. Sally now returns home after running a few miles to find the children dressed for school and Jim preparing the breakfast.

Letting go of the obsessive need for control meant doing less for the children, like staying out of their fights and allowing a child to sulk. Using Saturday morning for her ACOA meeting meant letting the children tend to themselves. At first they fought this, but when the old tactics of making their mother feel guilty no longer worked, they settled down to their own Saturday morning routines. As a consequence of this approach there are fewer fights, the children are calmer, and the anger in the household has diminished.

At her job Sally realized that being frantically busy was something she had created. Here again, the work of letting go of control meant talking and doing *less.* In managing other lawyers she learned to listen, rather than always use questions to direct conversations the way she wanted them to go. She found that it was not necessary to interfere with the work of other people, and learned to let them alone.

The same day I interviewed her she had had a committee meeting in which she had laughed a lot with the other people.

Her attitude toward these people had changed significantly since her first meeting with them a year earlier. At that time she considered them snobbish and prejudiced and thought that they were doing a poor job and that they knew much less than she, even though she was new to the committee. She came across antagonistically with them and could not get them to agree with her views. Her attitude a year later was to accept them with their limitations. She could say what she thought and accept that it was okay if they did not agree. It no longer meant they were bad people if they did not see things her way. She even accepted that they might know more than she.

Sally's attitude had changed over that year from harsh judgmentalism to one of acceptance. Part of her letting go of control and breaking her work addiction was taking Fridays off. This meant not only not going in to work, but not running errands and not fussing over the children. Her objective was to take some time each week for herself. At first she felt terrified at the unstructured time. She knew what she did not want to do, but had no idea what to do to relax and enjoy herself. This problem was solved by spending her Fridays at the ashram founded by Yogi Amrit Desai. She found his teachings to function as a "retooling." Having learned early in life "to do three things at once," she found that "focusing to quiet your mind and be fully present to what you are doing is a really different way of life."

Eventually, as Sally progresses with her recovery, it will be automatic for her to trust and respond to her feelings. At this stage, however, she must double-check her perceptions and judgments with her counselor and support group. This is the work involved in uncovering the attitudes and the behaviors that she can change. But the very process of doing this changed the most important relationship in her life, that with herself. As a result, her relationships with her husband, children, and coworkers underwent changes that reduced the anger in her life and gave her better health, more time to relax, and some peace of mind. As she learns to let go of her own obsessive need for control she finds that her relationships with the significant others in her life are more manageable.

CHAPTER 5

TRANSFORMATIONS

Inevitably, as your changing beliefs, attitudes, and behaviors are sorted out in terms of their consequences and your feelings, you will find yourself responding more automatically in self-actualizing ways. A transformation is a specific beneficial change in your behavior that occurs readily such that you find yourself substituting sane for dysfunctional behaviors with ease. Transformations signal the stage of recovery when you begin to experience some of the fruits of your labors.

No one can be expected to let go of control unless he or she feels safe. As you learn to make accurate judgments about how safe you are with other people and with various situations, you learn how to let go of the need for control. This sense of security depends on how safe you feel with your own feelings. If you are no longer overwhelmed by your new awareness of feelings, you can begin to look to them for the information they convey about how safe you are.

As you change behaviors, everyone you relate to notices the difference. Some will like it and offer you support; others will feel threatened and try to get you to revert to your old ways. Every such behavior change, even though beneficial, takes some getting used to and can disrupt a relationship.

While in the transformation stage you take on the challenge of dealing with disruptions in all your relationships.

For these reasons, and because adult children are so reluctant to yield control, there is a recommended strategy for bringing change into your life at this stage. First of all, you do not *have* to change. You do not have to do anything you do not yet feel comfortable with.

The Basic Strategy

The basic strategy of the transformations stage is, first, to check your feelings for the information they provide and, second, to chunk things down—to break things down into manageable "chunks." "Do I feel comfortable and safe with this person, situation, decision, or whatever?" is the first thing to check. Then ask yourself, "How can I chunk this down?" The idea is to break down the situation into specific steps that you feel safe taking one at a time. This is your antidote for the all-or-nothing functioning typical of adult children.

The strategy we call "share-check-share" is especially important when meeting new people or attempting to communicate with members of your family of origin. But it is almost always applicable in communicating with others. This is how it works. First, share whatever information about yourself you feel comfortable sharing. Check your listener's response. What is it, and how do you feel about it? If you feel safe about sharing some more, do it. At this point, do not tell your whole life story or all your thoughts and feelings about what is on your mind. Share some more information. Stop. Give your mouth a rest as your eyes, ears, and gut take in the other person's response. On the basis of how you feel about this you can continue the sharing, go on to another topic, or stop, i.e., terminate the conversation.

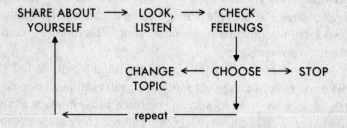

Anger

When it comes to dealing with anger, a variety of choices can be meaningful. If your problem has been that you bristle with anger and lash out at people, then you will feel encouraged when you find yourself acting calm in a provoking situation. If, on the other hand, you have always been afraid of your anger and repressed it as a bad feeling while mollifying others, you may take encouragement from a newly developed ability to express your anger appropriately.

Pat

Pat has always been a pugnaciously abrasive person. At the age of forty-two he found his marriage ended and his career as a legislative researcher in ruins. Although an unusually well-read and articulate person, he stated that describing his hostility was beyond words for him.

He remembered his parents as people who hated life and carried on intense battles with each other. They isolated from others and their fights were punctuated with horrific screaming and physical attacks. Toward Pat they expressed disappointment. "Why do you have to be such a failure?" said his father when Pat brought home his report cards. "How did I give birth to someone as inept as you?" His mother's comments were similar.

Pat went to work at the age of thirteen, when his father died, to try to assuage his mother's hysterical helplessness. His experience served only to reinforce his self-image as an unfortunate, mercilessly doomed failure. He has been obsessed with income as a measure of self-worth and consumed with resentment against the wealthy ever since. In fact, his resentment has been directed at anyone he perceives as more fortunate, which is almost everyone he knows.

As Pat worked his way through his first couple of years in recovery he managed to break out of his lifelong isolation, and developed a supportive network of men and women who accepted him. His participation in ACOA meetings allowed him to vent his feelings of hostility and pain. When I interviewed him he began in such a mood: "You are wasting your time interviewing me," he said. "I am one of the ones who simply don't make it." He was very reluctant to admit making any progress in his recovery.

But there is no doubt he has made progress. It is evident in his attitude and behavior. In the past, when Pat became annoyed at a public event he would stamp his feet, "huff and puff," move around, rustle things, grunt, and make disparaging comments under his breath as a prelude to an outburst of hostility. For example, he disrupted the reception after a wedding at which he had been an usher by telling the people at his table how much he despised them. He disrupted the tour of a mansion by pestering the guide with loaded questions about an "economic system that could allow people to spend their enormous wealth on such useless and gaudy things as a solid-gold bathtub." He disrupted his place of employment by publicly and vociferously telling his boss what a complete idiot he was. When I accompanied Pat to a public gathering a year prior to my interview with him, his angry mutterings provoked several people to suggest that he leave.

Pat has changed. At a recent dinner for which the audience had paid a fee to attend, he perceived that the featured speaker was "disgracefully unprepared." As the speaker rambled along Pat became increasingly upset by what he perceived as the man's arrogance. But he also noticed himself beginning to rustle things and move around restlessly. His annoyance energy was escalating. He interrupted it by asking the speaker a relevant question in a civil tone. The speaker was not able to answer the question, but continued rambling on. "I realized he had nothing to say," Pat recalled, "and I was able to detach from that, and just let it be." Instead of embarrassing the speaker with a series of caustic remarks, Pat chose to relax, let go of his expectations, and calm down.

What made this change in Pat's behavior significant as a transformation was that he realized he acted differently only after the incident had taken place. It had been an automatic and effortless decision on his part to let things be. It did not occur to him until he reflected on the incident that he had responded calmly to a situation that he always found extremely provoking. "Today I don't have to take all my pain and push it into somebody else's face," he said.

What made this behavior change easy for Pat was his new attitude. He no longer felt so threatened by the foibles of an authority figure that his annoyance had to escalate to a self-sabotaging outburst of anger. The consequences he enjoyed included acceptance by the people at the dinner and a sense of self-congratulation at his sane behavior. Since he had been unemployed for several years and wanted very much to get a job like the one he used to have, this transformation was important to him. He felt confident that he could function sensibly in the type of environment that used to drive him crazy. Attributing his past failures to his inability to learn from his mistakes, he finally felt that he understood how to get along with people.

As you let go of the obsessive need for control you automatically experience an uplifting of your self-esteem. The core belief underlying the control attitude is that you are helpless to protect yourself because you are no good and do not deserve to be protected. Pat's wounded inner child maintained this identity by acting out tantrums against what he perceived to be pompous authority figures. He used to tell the story of his mansion tour as a joke, with the punch line asserting that he was probably the only person in history to be kicked out of such a tour. This is a common adult child behavior, telling self-denigrating stories which convey the message, "I'm a jerk." Such a message is important to the wounded inner child; it confirms his choice to see himself as helpless and unworthy. But the years of acceptance experienced by Pat at ACOA meetings in which he bared his soul led to a self-acceptance that allowed him to act out sane behavior toward the dinner speaker.

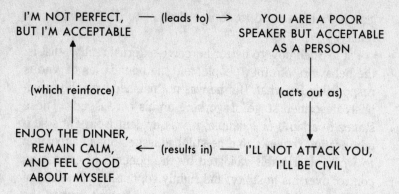

Pat experienced other such transformations taking place. They tend to come in bunches, and build a momentum. In addition to the consequences already mentioned, he experienced a sense of serenity, gratitude that the hard work done to let go of control had such beneficial results, and renewed hope in his recovery process. He saw a pattern emerging in his life around the issue of his annoyance that indicated he was learning to let go of his obsessive need for control.

The experience of such transformations will have several positive effects on you. They break through your cynicism about life with the message that you are getting better, healing is taking place, and it is okay to feel good about that. They allow the energy that used to be consumed by a particular self-belief-to-consequences syndrome to be freed up for your enjoyment. Such energy can give you a feeling of recuperation and renewed strength. After reviewing these changes in his life Pat felt better about himself, an experience I observed in everyone I interviewed. "Detaching with love is learning to accept the reality for whatever it is," he stated, "and learning what I need to do in order not to conflict with that reality."

Pat learned how to better perceive external reality, that is, the behaviors of other people, and the boundaries of who is responsible for what. But he was not finished with the previously described stage of working on his core issues. These stages overlap. For example, it was evident from Pat's self-deprecating remarks that he still had issues of self-alienation to work on. He felt validated by the benefits of exercising control over his hostility, and rightly so, but he still spoke of his life as being in ruins, expressed resentment toward the wealthy, and measured his self-worth in terms of his income, although not as strongly as before. He did not yet express an integrated vision of himself based on a sense of inner self-validation.

Catherine

Catherine, a physician, was introduced in Chapter 1 as a person who felt envious of those who could express themselves in the midst of a confrontation. Unlike Pat, she would freeze in the face of another's anger and become mute. She attributes this to her mother's constant warning about her father. "He's such a big man," she often repeated, "that if he ever got angry he would kill someone." Catherine never saw her father get angry and perpetrate physical violence, but she was thoroughly intimidated by her mother's fearfulness.

Her lifelong pattern was to melt in the face of anger and say or do whatever was necessary to mollify the other person. She witnessed a transformation in her behavior when a patient reacted to her recommendation for treatment with anger. The patient complained about the care she was receiving, stipulated the treatment she preferred, and used abusive language. "Godammit, you have to die around here before they'll take care of you," she shouted. Instead of freezing up with terror and apologizing, Catherine simply stated that her specification for treatment was based on her diagnosis, that what the patient demanded would not be denied her, but that it did not seem necessary. Then she added, "I really don't appreciate being sworn at." Her patient reacted by becoming more agitated with complaints and abusive language. Catherine told her she was free to seek care elsewhere, and the patient said she probably would.

In a confrontation such as this your anger is an important source of energy for setting boundaries and defining who you are. Catherine chose to not take responsibility for the other person's anger. She decided that she could not meet the other person's needs, not because she was inadequate, but because her patient was out of control. It was the patient's responsibility to discuss the issue of treatment in a reasonable way, and with respect. In fact, her patient was attempting to manipulate Catherine with her anger. Having put in much work on the issue of anger and control, Catherine was no longer naive about such behaviors and motivations.

Boundaries

Catherine's experience differed from Pat's in that she was confronted with another's anger aimed directly at her.

The patient was using blame tactics in an attempt to get Catherine to change her prescription. Such anger almost always triggers anger in the targeted person. In dysfunctional families anger spreads like a forest fire out of control, but the children are not permitted to express any such feeling toward the parents. A witness to Joel Steinberg's behavior, for example, recalled such an incident between father and daughter. Steinberg struck his daughter in the face, and then commanded, "Blink, and smile." The child obeyed. In Catherine's family also, as in Sue's, her parents would not permit her to express her anger at them. This deprived her of nature's way of delineating what was and was not acceptable to her. It is natural to get angry when slapped, criticized, yelled at, or ignored. When, as a child, the expression of your anger is squelched, and the feeling itself transformed into a magical thinking escape episode, you cannot develop a clear idea of who you are.

When you experience recovery as a gentle reparenting of yourself, allowing your natural anger to speak to you, you will feel a joyful affirmation of who you are. Your anger provides you with the information, and the energy you need, to establish and maintain boundaries. Catherine, for example, wanted to serve her patient conscientiously. She wanted to please her, to have her approval. When the patient objected to the way she was being treated, Catherine's first reaction, as an adult child, would be to placate her. But Catherine had trained herself, by working on her own core issue of control and anger, to recognize when her boundaries were being invaded. She was using the strategy of share-check-share or stop.

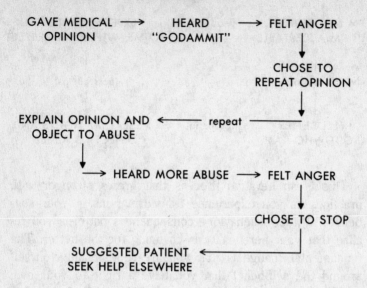

The key word in the above diagram is "chose." By consciously choosing what you are going to say and do you feel who you are. Your choice is based on your own feeling, which is information about what you like and do not like. You do not act out your anger by blaming the other person, but you acknowledge it as realistic information about what your limitations and boundaries are. You can bypass the magical thinking of your inner wounded child, gently reassuring him or her that such thinking was okay in childhood because it was necessary to survive, and feel your energy released into a joyful acknowledgment of who you really are. Finally, you can affirm this experience by sharing it with your support network, your "family of choice," and receiving their congratulations on your growth as a person. All this energy reinforces your growing belief that you are basically okay as a human being.

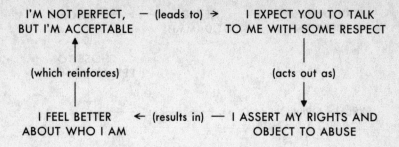

This is an iterative process that grows stronger with practice. As you experience transformations in your self-belief → attitude → behavior → consequences patterns you realize that your personality is changing for the better. The fundamental change is that you are reorganizing yourself around the self-belief that you have a right to your own existence, to be who you are capable of being. Each transformation lets you know that a specific dysfunctional pattern in your life has been healed, and the energy formerly trapped in that syndrome is available to empower your further growth. You will then become more sensitive to another dysfunctional pattern, something you were unaware of, and will focus your attention on that as your next core issue.

Many people compare this process to removing the layers of an onion. As each layer is peeled away a new one appears. I prefer Yogi Amrit Desai's analogy to peeling away the layers of tape from around a light bulb. The inner light and warmth of your natural life force, with its innate needs and universal intelligence, shines forth more strongly and guides you more confidently as each layer of dysfunction is stripped away.

Bill

Bill's experience of a transformation shows how understanding your wounded inner child can help heal the fragmented ego states of your personality. Bill's family dysfunction included a belligerent father who could erupt into violence at any time. As the oldest of five children, Bill took on the responsibility of caring for his siblings from an early age. But his sense of inner integrity was fragmented by his need to survive his father's punishing explosions. Since his father would never hit a particular younger sister because she was retarded, Bill developed the habit of blaming her for whatever his father got angry about. Surviving created such torment within him that he came close to self-destructing completely at the age of twenty-five.

At the age of thirty-six, after four years in recovery as an adult child of a dysfunctional family, Bill related to people quite differently from a few years previously. For example, he had recently asked his boss for a month off so he could go away for codependency treatment and for a loan to help pay the cost. His boss gladly agreed. With a former employer Bill had grown a beard in defiance of company policy simply to act out his rebelliousness. The consequences had been humiliating for him.

A workshop that Bill attended a year previously included a rebirthing exercise. Rebirthing involves rapid and prolonged breathing while in a prone position to induce an emotionally conscious connection with birth and infancy experiences. Bill's way of implementing the basic strategy of share-check-share/stop was to consult with his inner child. "That's how I do things in my life now," he said. "I stay in touch with my little kid, and say, 'Are you ready to do this? Can you handle it?' "

This "little kid" that he refers to has been identified as an ego state within him that embodies his fears. This ego state was given the name "little Billie." This technique allowed Bill to talk to himself and to express himself to a trusted friend. With such a friend Bill talked about whether he wanted to undergo the rebirthing experience or not. By saying things like "Little Billie says he isn't ready for this, he can't handle it," Bill was expressing his fears in a self-respecting way. He would feel embarrassed to admit as an adult man that he was afraid to do what everyone else in the workshop was doing. But by personifying his fears as "Little Billie" and treating this part of himself with the respect and gentleness due any child, he experienced a more loving acknowledgment and acceptance of who he was.

As an adult child you need to do this sort of thing to honestly acknowledge your painful feelings without your inner critical parent tearing you to pieces for doing so. To Bill this was not just an intellectual technique. He used photos of himself as a young child, and constant inner dialogue, to help identify emotionally with that part of himself that had to survive an insanely belligerent father.

Shortly before I interviewed Bill he had attended a rebirthing workshop and done the breathing exercise. But that was not the basis for his feeling good about himself and for his increased sense of self-esteem. What he felt good about was that he had acknowledged, expressed, and respected his fears and had chosen to wait until he felt ready to handle the experience. This is different from feeling good about an external happening such as receiving money or the approval of another person. The feeling goes deeper because in this type of experience you are connecting with some deep inner belief about yourself and turning the negative into a positive by accepting yourself as you are.

I have tried everything I know of to achieve this in myself, and have found no approach more powerful than visualizing my core negative belief syndromes as personified by the different children I was when I had to make such adaptations to survive. I am now speaking in the plural because, as mentioned in Chapter 2, different types of abuse and neglect give rise to a variety of survival ego states.

An Example of Personality Fragmentation

For example, "Den" is that part of me who knows he can never do anything right, and even if he did something right, the only result he must expect and prepare for would be a brutal punishment. He is my inner wounded child, and the world he lives in is a nightmare. If he were politically empowered to create a world in which he could feel secure, he would employ the same Gestapo techniques that another adult child of an alcoholic once organized in Nazi Germany. Fighting this part of myself with blame and denial results in self-loathing and behaviors that bring about a reinforcing of the idea that I should be punished and destroyed. Accepting this part of me with heartfelt appreciation for the pain Den had to endure and the "magic" he employed to survive helps to stop the festering resentments and heal the wounds inflicted so long ago in my life.

I have identified many other such ego states, and personified them with names. The part of me that would exercise control like an aggressive policeman wielding his billy club I call "the Bruiser." This, in fact, was the nickname given me

135

in high school because of my aggressive style of play on the soccer field. A character you would much rather meet is the witty and charming Irishman I can be when I want to relax, have a good time, and not allow unpleasant thoughts or personalities to interfere. I actually speak with a brogue and adopt a completely different personality when in this mode. This part of me is named "Father O'Malley," after the character played by Bing Crosby in *The Bells of St. Mary's.*

You would rather have "the Bruiser" on your team than on the opposing team, and you would probably enjoy meeting "Father O'Malley" at a party. In my recovery process they both personify core issues, anger and the fear underlying approval seeking, respectively. Part of their purpose is to see to it that you never suspect that "Den" exists, because he personifies my most painful core issue, that of my own sense of self-worth.

Recovery then, through the stages explained thus far, is a repetitive process of working on and resolving a variety of core issues, personified as inner children. As transformations develop into new patterns in your life, you can use the freed-up energy they represent to go to the core of who your wounded inner child is, and bring the healing process to him or her. Many core issues may be involved, but a simplified diagram of this process shows how core issues are related to transformations.

Resolving core issues means choosing to understand and accept yourself with love, and as a consequence experiencing transformations. Each such choice strengthens your growing identity. Who is making the choice, your wounded inner child? Some other ego state? No, they are not capable of such choices. Only you, with the identity you are creating, have the capability of making such conscious choices.

"The Bruiser" (Core Issue: Anger)

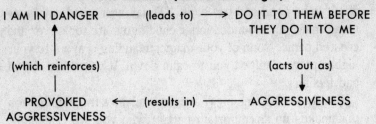

I AM IN DANGER —— (leads to) ——→ DO IT TO THEM BEFORE
THEY DO IT TO ME

↑ (which reinforces) | (acts out as)

PROVOKED ←—— (results in) —— AGGRESSIVENESS
AGGRESSIVENESS

WHEN RESOLVED

"Father O'Malley" (Core Issue: Fear)

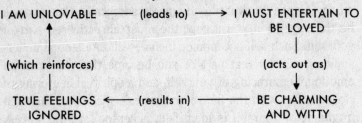

I AM UNLOVABLE —— (leads to) ——→ I MUST ENTERTAIN TO
BE LOVED

↑ (which reinforces) | (acts out as)

TRUE FEELINGS ←—— (results in) —— BE CHARMING
IGNORED AND WITTY

WHEN RESOLVED

"Den" (Core Issue: Pain)

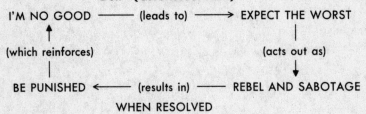

I'M NO GOOD —— (leads to) ——→ EXPECT THE WORST

↑ (which reinforces) | (acts out as)

BE PUNISHED ←—— (results in) —— REBEL AND SABOTAGE

WHEN RESOLVED

ME (Core Issue: Who I Choose to Be)

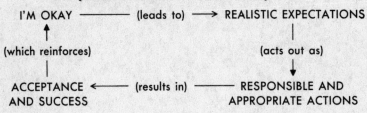

I'M OKAY —— (leads to) ——→ REALISTIC EXPECTATIONS

↑ (which reinforces) | (acts out as)

ACCEPTANCE ←—— (results in) —— RESPONSIBLE AND
AND SUCCESS APPROPRIATE ACTIONS

If you participate in support meetings you may often talk about your good and bad days. "Today was a bad day" may mean that your wounded inner child ego state took over and created panic. None of your magic, including prayers to your higher power, helped you to calm down. It was a bad day of bad feelings.

But these "bad feelings" are themselves a fragment of you that makes up an important part of who you are. Talking it out at a meeting helps salve the wounds with acceptance. You may talk a lot about how you hope to love yourself someday when you are recovered enough. Paradoxically, that day will be the day when you accept the most unrecovered part of yourself. Such self-acceptance includes an intellectual understanding of why that part of you became the way it is, an emotional embracing of yourself, and a spiritual centering of closer union with the life force that energizes you. As each fragment of yourself is identified, accepted, and embraced, you eventually emerge as an adult with an integrated personality.

CHAPTER 6

INTEGRATION

At some point in the process of working on core issues and undergoing transformations, you experience a change that is not just another typical transformation. This change is different from the others in that it takes place at a deeper level of your self-belief system. It brings to full consciousness the realization that it really is okay to love yourself exactly as you are, that you do not have to wait till you are perfectly recovered.

When this realization is heartfelt and your mind is quietly open to it, you become flooded with a self-validating warmth. You *feel* your self-love, and as a consequence of being keenly responsive to your own feelings, you experience the enjoyment of being loved and accepted for who you are. As a result, your previously fragmented personality begins the process of integrating around the experience of self-acceptance.

Your wounded inner child still hurts, still feels anger, and is still inclined to act out in dysfunctional ways. But the key transformation you experience is that you consciously accept this part of yourself and cease fighting it. You realize that by fighting your negative self-beliefs you have been abusing your wounded inner child with self-criticism and perfectionistic impatience, just as your parents did. It may seem paradoxical, but once accepted and assured of your unconditional love, your inner child no longer has to get attention by acting out its attitudes of blame and denial. On the contrary, the daily practice of self-acceptance evolves into a continually more enjoyable experience of yourself. The wisdom of unconditional self-acceptance replaces magical thinking as your basis for perceiving and interacting with others.

Many people I have talked to state that they are at or beyond the stage of integration. "I know who I am and what I want," they tell me. "I know where I'm going." They state this with such conviction that there is little room left for doubt. But further conversation and behavior often fail to substantiate this assertion.

Integration means that your body, mind, and emotions are mutually supportive in self-caring ways. You do not poison your blood, for example with substances like sugar, disrupt your nervous system with caffeine, and numb your feelings with nicotine. You sleep and exercise with regularity so that you are rested and vigorous. You eat whatever foods you know to be most beneficial for you and avoid those that are not. You love your body as your physical self, with too much respect willfully to abuse or neglect it in any way.

This respectful caring for your physical self reflects a mental attitude that you bring to your relating with other people. Whether in the workplace or with family members, friends, or a significant other, you are self-accepting and self-caring. You experience a full range of emotions, joy as well as anger, serenity as well as sadness. You know that this is not just another good mood that may last for a week or so, with the accompanying anxiety about how long it will last. Chronic anxiety dissipates, and you no longer experience panic attacks.

Integration does not happen overnight. It is a gradual process that takes hold as a result of your working on your core issues and experiencing transformations within the context of a supportive group. It develops through phases and is comparable in its results to a healthy adolescence (see Chapter 1). By the end of the process you know who you are and are confident of making this identity known to others.

The following examples show how individuals develop positive self-belief systems around their feelings of self-acceptance and how they no longer tolerate mistreatment or thoughtless behavior.

Joan

The early phase of integration is exemplified by Joan, who is experiencing her developing self-identity and growing sense of self-esteem as the new power in her life. At the age of thirty-five, after five years in recovery, Joan's personal priorities are developed to the point where she can present herself to people as the imperfect human being she is, rather than as the superachiever who could take care of everyone and, at work, solve all her employer's problems.

The youngest of five children, she had taken on the hero role at fourteen when her mentally ill mother died, leaving her the only girl at home to take care of her obsessively resentful father. She endured covert sexual abuse from him as he eavesdropped on her during visits from her boyfriend, kissed her on the mouth when leaving, and came into her bedroom one night. The legacy of blame and denial that was hers from early childhood led her to seek approval as a straight-A student, and later as a workaholic employee. She described her career during her twenties as jobs with very demanding and critical bosses who had panic situations requiring her to "save everybody."

Her addictions to food and romance brought about her awakening at age thirty. With her roommate she spent evenings and weekends smoking marijuana, eating, and watching television, until she was a "235-pound couch potato." When a new boyfriend whom she hoped would be her Prince Charming absconded after "borrowing" a substantial sum of money, she realized it was time to get control of her life. Her recovery began with Overeaters Anonymous meetings, and later included psychoanalysis and ACOA. Through her recovery she succeeded in reducing her weight to a healthy and attractive level, eliminated alcohol and drugs from her lifestyle, and quit smoking.

For Joan, recovery consists of making choices, accepting the consequences, evaluating her alternatives, and learning from her experiences. She shares her experiences honestly with two old friends, as well as with a growing network of new ones. Her basic operating self-belief is that she is too good as a person to have to accept abuse and neglect. Her overriding attitude is that it is more important to grow as a person and to be honest with herself and others in her relationships than to acquire the status-oriented things that used to make up her agenda. She actively seeks out people who can be supportive of her desire to develop friendships based on honesty and the shared values of self-caring and mutual respect. As a result, she is able to construct, maintain, and develop a lifestyle that she finds healthy and enjoyable. Her newly evolved pattern can be diagrammed thus:

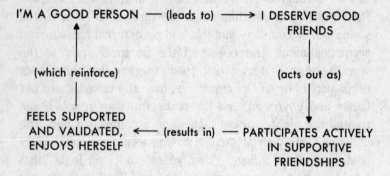

I'M A GOOD PERSON — (leads to) ——→ I DESERVE GOOD FRIENDS

(which reinforce)   (acts out as)

FEELS SUPPORTED
AND VALIDATED, ←— (results in) — PARTICIPATES ACTIVELY
ENJOYS HERSELF   IN SUPPORTIVE
                                 FRIENDSHIPS

This pattern is evident in the choices she made recently in her personal relationships. After living with a man for a year and working patiently with him on his issues of jealousy and possessiveness, she decided to ask her partner to leave. This decision was based on her desire to have a supportive relationship rather than one in which her energy went into constantly mothering the wounded inner child of her lover. Joan then had to deal with her anxieties around giving up the sexual gratification of this relationship and dealing with the financial management of the lease they had shared on the house in which she lived. "But," she said, "once I made the choice to get out of a bad relationship, the logistics were not difficult."

As she related this experience, Joan wondered aloud whether this was an example of her self-esteem growing stronger. Her conclusion emphasized the self-validation typical of people in the integration stage of recovery when she stated, "I don't know what it is, but I sure do like it."

Her confidence in basing decisions on gut instincts was further strengthened by her choice of a new roommate. Rather than rely on things like the prospect's résumé, the status of her company and job, and on external measures of accomplishment, she observed the personal style of the woman she was interviewing. Joan observed that she did not drink alcohol or smoke cigarettes, how she talked about her family and boyfriend, and the respectful way in which she treated the eight-year-old niece who accompanied her. The individual was very attractive, having won a national beauty contest while in college. "Two years ago," said Joan, "that would have been an excuse to hate her." But Joan's gut told her that this woman was a person of integrity, someone who wanted to live a good life rather than acquire things. Her decision to accept this person as her roommate resulted in a mutually supportive and friendly relationship that she continues to enjoy.

In establishing new friendships Joan took the initiative to reach out to people and get to know them. Through a women's book discussion club she joined, and by following up on otherwise casual acquaintances, she has managed to meet several career women her age who, like her, are single. For example, after meeting a woman while getting her nails done, she called this new acquaintance to invite her to have dinner and see a play together. "I've never done that before," she said. It is typical of people experiencing the integration brought on by self-acceptance that they reach out to others not only for help, but to share their appreciation of life.

On her job Joan is reevaluating her career goals. Employed as the regional purchasing manager for an international fast-food chain, she ran into conflict with her boss when she refused to credit the account of a dominant franchisee for a mistake he had made. When this man refused to pay for some promotional items he had purchased but not used, the only way the corporation could get reimbursed was to bill everyone else in a covert manner. "Add a penny a pound on fries, and you get the money back from everybody else," Joan explained. Unwilling to implement this policy, she was confronted by an angry boss over her "stupidity." To help herself deal with this painful situation Joan relied on sharing her experience with her friends, and accepting responsibility for the consequences of her decisions. She also admitted to eating too much candy at business meetings, allowing the sugar to palliate her anger.

Joan did not find support for her values in her workplace and endured an angry tirade from her boss. Committed as she is to making her own choices and accepting the consequences, she is reviewing this experience with her friends and thinking about alternatives to her present job.

Joan was not fully integrated at the time I interviewed her, but was not waiting for that to occur to love and accept herself and to share herself honestly with others. She was in the process of integrating her physical, mental, and emotional aspects in mutually supportive, self-caring ways. She was physically vigorous and attractive and knew that her penchant for eating candy was a sign of stress. She was mentally aware of her growth process and of what she wanted to do to take care of herself physically and emotionally. She was emotionally stable and connected with a network of friends on whom she could rely for support and mutual enjoyment.

Gus

Gus felt integration as a new power he had begun to exercise in his life. "My problem," he stated, "was thinking what ACOA taught me but feeling what my childhood taught me. I've been able to integrate the two." By diligently sharing his thoughts and feelings at meetings and consciously working through the long-repressed feelings of his childhood, he has developed his ability to choose for himself. As a child Gus was neglected by his parents to the point that he never developed any identity other than that of the follower who would do anything to gain the approval of others. At the age of forty-three, after four years of recovery meetings and therapy, he also exemplified an early phase of integration.

His former level of codependency was demonstrated by an incident typical of his relationship with his girlfriend, Sandy. He recalled driving her car over to his place a few years ago to wash it and change the oil. Before leaving her house he had told her he might just as well take her laundry along and do that also. He spent the entire afternoon washing and waxing her car, changing the oil, and doing two loads of her laundry. At sunset he was feeling very tired as he arrived back at Sandy's to see his own car sitting in her yard, "all filthy, and needing an oil change," and realized his own laundry was still unwashed. Emphasizing the change he has undergone, he stated, "Today I take care of my own needs first."

Taking care of his own needs began with a realization that he had to take responsibility for his physical health as a way of caring for himself. He had high cholesterol and found himself depending completely on his girlfriend to buy and prepare the right foods. He saw his codependency manifested in this as he realized he would go through the trouble of researching, shopping for, and cooking the right foods for her, or "anybody else," but not for himself. "I decided that I needed to be the most important person in my life," he asserted, and chose to move away from the person who was enabling his codependency. He had been living by himself for about half a year when I interviewed him, and was finding a new satisfaction in doing all the daily chores required for self-care.

Gus's new determination to take care of himself physically led him to insist that his boss stop smoking cigars in his presence, a behavior directly opposite to his longstanding approval-seeking pattern. He recalled that he had mentioned to his boss several times the fact that the cigar fumes gave him headaches, with consequent loss of sleep. Gus had requested that he not smoke while they were together. Recently, while talking in the office, his boss had pulled out a cigar to light it. Gus simply said to him, "I don't need this job if it's going to upset my health," and left. His boss came after him to apologize and promised to refrain from smoking in his presence.

Like Joan, Gus can be compared to a person forming an identity in the course of a healthy adolescence. Both of them had recently ended live-in relationships with a person of the opposite sex, acknowledging that they were not yet ready for a fully committed relationship and that they needed time to develop their own sense of self. This is an important step for adult children in recovery because it frees them from the basic syndrome of the codependent, who believes that he or she can find self-worth only through the acceptance of a significant other.

Gus preferred to widen his circle of friends, exercising his share-check-share/stop strategy with a growing sense of self-confidence. When, for example, a new friend ignored him during a party to which she had invited him, he asked her what was wrong. She acknowledged that she felt attracted to him and was not sure how to handle her feelings. This gave Gus a clearer understanding of what was going on and helped him avoid spending his energy wondering what he might be doing to displease her and how he should act to gain her approval. He saw that his friend may have a problem dealing with her feelings, but that there was no need to take it on as his own problem. Avoiding such a drain on his mental energy supported his focus to take care of his own needs.

Gus saw the turning point in his recovery when he realized that he had the knowledge he had sought so arduously and that it was time to put it into daily practice. For years he read several recovery books at a time and attended as many as five meetings a week, constantly looking for the solutions to the problems and crises of his life. He practiced the exercises recommended for recovery such as honestly sharing his thoughts and feelings to supportive others, building a network of friends he could trust, and following the guidance of a knowledgeable therapist. Now he has what he calls "a whole different outlook." "I don't wake up each morning wondering if I'm going to find the answer," he stated. "I already know the answers. It is really exciting to be in charge of my life, and to meet people without the fear of someone taking over my life."

His basic operating belief was that he had the knowledge and the tools to live by his own agenda and that his own needs were his top priority. This gave rise to an attitude of self-confidence and a sense of being in charge of his life. He acted this confidence out by setting boundaries with himself and with others. For example, in addition to taking care of his own nutritional needs, he played tennis regularly, enjoyed his scooter, and refused to work weekends on his job as a handyman. As a result he felt empowered every time he asserted himself, and respected his self-identity as it grew stronger. "I feel the happiest that I have ever been," he stated. His new pattern looks like this diagram:

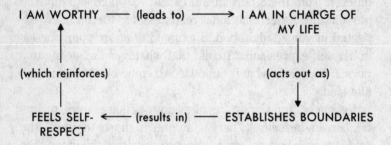

Gus worked very hard for years on his recovery. I remember many meetings where he shared with amazing detail the self-doubts, fears, and worries that constantly afflicted his mind. He deserves the peace of mind he now enjoys, and no one knows that better than he.

Candy

Candy exemplifies a later phase of the integration process, comparable to the adolescent soon to embark on young adulthood. The integration process may continue for a year or two as self-acceptance deepens, but those experiencing it no longer suffer the degree of doubt and impatience typical of previous stages in recovery. In Chapter 1, Candy illustrated the strong sense of self-acceptance that underlies her integration, and her survival syndrome was diagrammed in Chapter 2. You may recall that the self-belief that she was crazy resulted in a pattern of self-sabotaging behaviors and feelings of hopelessness. After five years of dedicated recovery work she had a very strong sense of who she was. Having experienced the integration process for a year longer than Joan and Gus, she differed from them only in the extent to which she enjoyed herself and in her emotional readiness for the intimacy expected in young adulthood. She could be more spontaneous in her self-expression. "I trust that whatever I'm saying to a person is exactly what is supposed to come out at that time," she said.

Recovery, for Candy, resulted in a genuine spirit of joyfulness in herself. "There's so much more to life," she said, "than being an adult who had a rotten childhood. I'm very creative and loving. I have a playful spirit. I'm very highly motivated, and what is nice is that the more recovery and self-love I have, the more people I draw into my life."

Her joy gave her added courage in making decisions based on what she felt she wanted for herself. For example, she recently refused a part-time job for a woman she had worked for in the past. After meeting with this person to discuss what the work would entail, she consulted her feelings and acknowledged to herself that the work was too time-consuming, and the employer too intimidating. Candy called her the next day to tell her simply, "I don't want to do this." This kind of straightforward assertion is its own reward to the person experiencing integration. It is a manifestation of the individual's identity; simultaneously, it determines a course of action that enhances rather than sabotages her life. Candy was aware that the employer could hire somebody else to do the work, and that taking it on would cramp her lifestyle unnecessarily. Her bottom line was the statement that "I am not going to give up some of my play time to do this involved work." Giving herself this kind of consideration has a healing effect on her inner wounded child. It enables the wounds to heal and the child to grow.

She described her integration by saying that her body and mind were more connected. If she felt an ache in her stomach, or pains, or fatigue, she interpreted her bodily messages as guidelines for taking care of herself. She found that her feelings got more intense as she progressed in recovery. Whatever the feelings were, whether joy or sadness, she could welcome them as manifestations of herself. "The joys are deeper, and so is the sadness, but it leaves sooner," she stated. "I understand the process of letting the feeling go through my body, and when it is gone I'm in the next moment. All my feelings are good because when I am feeling them I am living."

Like others at this stage of recovery, Candy put a high priority on taking good care of herself physically, seeing to it that she got proper food, exercise, and quiet time. Her physical reactions were interpreted as indications of her emotional needs. She expressed this as a manifestation of her hard-won self-esteem. "I love myself too much today to get off center," she said.

She knows how to meditate to find the answers she needs within herself, and how to ask others for help. This knowledge is the major asset acquired in recovery. I must emphasize again that it is an asset when it is emotionally based in experience, and not merely intellectual. It manifests itself in knowing how to achieve and maintain the balance needed for living a centered life. Remember that although I am comparing the stage of integration with the developmental stage of healthy adolescence, the recovery process for adult children requires *unlearning* dysfunctional patterns, and consciously letting go of resistance to the pain this entails. "In the beginning this balance was real hard to get, and it took time," Candy testified.

A major project Candy was implementing when I first interviewed her was her decision to relocate from an Eastern metropolitan area to a small town in the West. Since adult children sometimes relocate in search of the "geographical cure" of their problems, I was interested in her reasons for moving and her method of proceeding. The "geographical cure" is an attempt to escape the pain of emotional chaos in one's life by moving to a location that seems to have a more agreeable climate, "friendlier people," or a more easygoing lifestyle. More often than not, such a move involves illusions rather than preparations, and results in increased isolation rather than any kind of "cure."

But Candy had visited the place she wanted to move to, had lived there for a while, had a close friend living there, and had made contacts for the establishment of a support network. She had formed a perception of what the community was like and what her employment options were, which was based on the experience of living there and interacting with people. Her decision to relocate came over a period of a year as she allowed herself to open to the attraction of a small-town lifestyle.

Moving required that she sell her house, and she found

152

the many friends she had made in her recovery to be most helpful. These friends included a real estate agent, an accountant, and a lawyer, to whom she went for advice and information. "I want to sell my house, and I feel really inadequate," she told her friend in the real estate business. "What should I do?" Receiving all the information she needed, she experienced the empowerment of being able to acknowledge her limitations, obtain the assistance she needed, and thus get beyond the limits that would otherwise constrain her.

I know from my own experience that it is by acknowledging my limitations and letting go of the need to be in control of everything that I find the means of living beyond the limits they would otherwise impose. Candy's experience shows how easy it is to do this, once she had learned to trust reliable people with her concerns.

Like Joan and Gus, Candy expressed her belief that her life is a good one, that the trauma of her painful childhood is behind her. Her belief that she was crazy has been replaced by love of self. "Today I love myself exactly where I am at every given moment, most of the time," she stated enthusiastically. She expressed this as a deep gratitude for the personality change she had experienced in her recovery. "I never imagined that it would really happen," she said, "but it has, and it's better than I dreamed." Having been superresponsible most of her life, she valued her sense of responsibility as an asset, but was now more joyful and warm in her interactions with people and able to share her playfulness and spontaneity. "I play very well at a lot of different things," she said, referring to her ability to have fun and play with friends in noncompetitive ways. As a result she found more people attracted to her, and her life became enriched with friends.

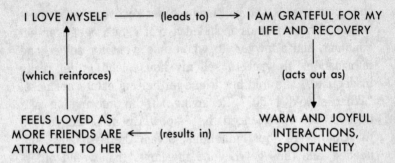

Candy continues to grow and expand the range of people with whom she can relate in mutually supportive ways and within whatever limits she deems appropriate. She expressed heartfelt gratitude for her recovery, referring to it as a "miracle." "I never thought I could get through the pain of my early stages in recovery," she said. "I thought I would always be an adult child, with the weight of fear and self-hatred always on my back. But it's not anymore."

Summary

Joan, Gus, and Candy all exemplify the mutually self-caring commitment of their physical, mental, and emotional selves that constitutes their sense of personal identity. They each take pleasure in sharing this identity with other people at work and in their personal lives. Joan was experiencing tension on her job because values she was identifying with more strongly were in conflict with corporate policies that she was expected to implement. It was evident from her testimony that her hard-won priorities of self-caring were leading her away from a job that served priorities she no longer valued.

Gus was more assertive on his job, feeling secure enough to risk it if it continued to hamper his health or invade his boundaries. Candy's self-confidence in her ability to relate to people successfully overrode any concern she may have had about employment.

All of them were fully aware of how the characteristics typical of adult children had manifested themselves in their lifestyles prior to experiencing integration. Daily practice of consulting with their feelings and discussing their issues with supportive friends had become an automatic part of their living strategies. Fear of people was no longer inhibiting them because it no longer made sense to their positive self-belief systems. Approval-seeking behaviors had been replaced by self-approval seeking, as their own bodily, mental, and emotional signals became the important messages to which they responded. Feelings of self-alienation were no longer credible since these people liked who they were and could accept themselves with their past as well as their present lives. Fun and intimacy were part of their regular enjoyments in life since both these experiences must be felt with others, and much of their energy was devoted to sharing themselves with other people.

I found it interesting and significant that none of them was involved in an intimate relationship with a significant other at this stage, but had in fact ended such relationships. Being codependent and prone to isolation, the relationships they had ended were actually blocks to enjoying intimacy with people. They were all acutely aware that enjoying the growing intimacy they experienced with themselves would eventually lead to intimacy with a significant other, in due time. They were not in any hurry about such a development. The anxiety caused by the inner emptiness of the adult child syndrome was no longer driving them to seek validation in the arms of another.

The mature self-commitment that seeks to express itself in the mutual commitment of emotional and sexual intimacy, typical of the young adult stage of development, is the eventual outcome of integration. It manifests itself in the next stage of recovery, Genesis.

CHAPTER 7

GENESIS

Genesis is the stage of recovery in which the individual experiences and expresses a healthy and creative self-actualization. This level of maturity is comparable to the young adult stage of normal growth described by Erikson (see Chapter 1). In tune with your natural talents, personal values, and integrated identity, you simply live your life as you see fit. The observable consequences at this stage include all those of the previous stage—physical, mental, and emotional self-caring that structures your relating with others—plus a readiness for intimacy with others in close relationships, including sexual union. The criterion on which I chose to rely for determining whether individuals were experiencing genesis was whether or not they were able to develop and maintain their own identity while participating in an intimate relationship involving sexual union with a person of the opposite sex.

This type of relationship was expressed by almost everyone I interviewed as the desirable outcome of their efforts in recovery. Those who were at the integration stage, however, were in no hurry to have such a relationship in their lives. They were keenly aware of the need to allow themselves a year or two to grow into their newly integrating identities and to become more comfortable with themselves before engaging in intimacy with a person of the opposite sex.

I have observed others at meetings in which I participate who pair off in couples long before they reach integration. Some are people getting divorced after long marriages who find comfort with each other, others have been single for quite some time and simply respond to a strong sexual attraction. In every case I have observed a good measure of magical thinking at work cloaking sexual neediness with romance, a tendency to isolate from others, and an interruption of the work on core issues. Such relationships signal a regression to survival strategies and present the individuals in them with one of the toughest issues they will have to work on, namely the adult child addiction to sex and romance. This issue awaits them once the magical thinking, such as "My life is so wonderful now that I have a supportive, understanding partner," wears thin. If the basic reason for being close to someone else is that you cannot stand being by yourself, then your relationship is codependent.

The genesis stage of recovery finds you capable of and ready for intimacy without codependency, and sexual gratification without the lust that has no respect for personal boundaries. Two of the thirty-five people I interviewed are at this stage in their recoveries. Their testimonies serve to illustrate quite clearly how they work at the intimacy they enjoy with their sexual partner, and how this part of their lives fits in with the rest. What emerges is a picture of the integrated person exercising his or her sense of self in the domain of emotional intimacy with a significant other.

Since everyone I talked with had experienced survival and at least some degree of emergent awareness, it could be expected that fewer people would be at the more advanced stages. I had hoped, however, to find more than two people at the stage of genesis, and advertised and networked for a year in my search. It soon became evident that the number of years one spends in a "recovery program" are not an indication of recovery, since many people revert to survival tactics and prolong codependent relationships with others, including their therapists. But the two people I found satisfied my need to get an accurate insight into the day-to-day nature of this level of recovery and to validate the criterion of intimacy within a sexual relationship as its expression.

Candy

When I first interviewed Candy she was experiencing integration, as described in the previous chapter. Having an intimate relationship was not one of the things on her mind at that time, since she was relocating. But when I interviewed her again more than a year and a half later, she had been intimately involved with a man for a year. At the age of thirty-one, having been divorced for over five years, she had been able to bring the trust experienced in her recovery process to her relationship with a man. This trust expressed itself in the honest sharing of her feelings, as well as her thoughts, with a man who was capable of doing the same with her.

The most salient feature of her relationship with her friend was the communication, based on their feelings, that they conscientiously maintained. Candy is certainly not repeating the dysfunctional patterns that created the emotional chaos in her previous relationships, based as they were on the model of her aggressively alcoholic father and codependent mother. Her description of this relationship bears witness to the significant changes that have taken place in her personality and to the power of the recovery process.

She met her friend, Kendall, shortly after arriving at her new home. The brother of her girlfriend, he accompanied them to a concert. He had been looking forward to Candy's arrival since meeting her at a party the year before and observing her interact with other people. Since he had attended the party with his two young children and a woman friend, Candy had not taken much notice of him. But he had expressed his interest in Candy by repeatedly asking his sister during the ensuing months, "When is your friend moving out here?"

Candy recalled that when she met Kendall to attend the concert she felt an immediate connection with him, that something about him "touched her soul." "It wasn't sexual in the sense that I wanted to go to bed with him right away," she said. "I know what lust is. This was something different." There was a sense of relaxation between them, a calm understanding that they were very much alike. As Candy put it, "He's like the male me."

Two days later he called her to tell her how he was feeling, and that he wanted to see her again. His honesty and vulnerability attracted her. She felt safe and excited. "My God," she thought, "is he for real?" But she was afraid that things had happened too fast, and so she spent the next six months getting to know her new friend by sharing her feelings, checking his responses, and deciding whether she wanted to continue with him. She loved the way he was able to listen to her and accept what she had to say without analyzing it or trying to fix her. She found herself spending more and more time with him, until a routine was established of spending their evenings together at a variety of activities. For example, on

Mondays they attended the same ACOA meeting, on Tuesdays went to a dance class, and so on.

Eventually they began to feel smothered by this routine, and each wondered, separately, what to do about it. "I'm feeling scared to talk about this," Kendall said one night. "I'm feeling kind of smothered. We've gotten into this habit of planning things all week long, and I don't have any time to myself." Candy listened to what he had to share, allowed her feelings to be with her, and then expressed them. "I feel relieved," she said, "because I've been thinking the same thing but didn't want to say anything right away. I don't want to plan so many things together all the time."

As a result of this conversation they felt closer, and did not in fact significantly reduce the time they spent together. It had been difficult to share their thoughts about feeling smothered in their relationship, but confronting their fear and expressing it honestly had resulted in an even stronger appreciation for each other. They both took self-acceptance within the dynamic of honest sharing as the measure of the value of their relationship, and their confidence in the relationship grew stronger. As their sharing became more intimate, they were able to create boundaries and guidelines for themselves to encourage their continued free expression within the safety of mutually assured acceptance.

This practice of communicating through feelings of fear was exemplified in many other instances recounted by Candy, with feelings of sadness, neediness, anger, and disappointment being similarly expressed. Each such sharing brought them closer and as time went by, made it easier to repeat such interactions. The main reason for this is that both took responsibility for their feelings. "We don't blame each other," Candy said, "we don't look to each other to fix anything. We talk about our feelings, express them, and let them go. There is a lot of mutual acceptance, and I never had that before in a relationship with a man."

As a result of this kind of sharing they have grown relaxed enough to draw out the playfulness in each other. Having fun together is a major source of enjoyment in their relationship. If they feel like acting silly and uninhibited they can do so, and know how to validate each other without obsessing about the approval of others. It is as if each gives the other permission to come out and play.

When they eventually began to express their intimacy through sexual sharing, their sexual experiences could reflect and express the comfort they felt in communicating with each other, and the uninhibited playfulness they enjoyed together. When they talked about their sexual experiences afterward instead of saying, "Was it good for you?" or "Did you like it?" they asked, "What did you like about it?" and "What didn't you like about it?" "Our conversations about our sex life," said Candy, "are the same as about other things, like buying groceries, or whatever." Rather than assume that the other person would know what they wanted, they developed the habit of asking for what they needed and telling the other what they liked and wanted while making love. This developed gradually out of their talks about sex afterward, and their agreement to make it a rule that each would be responsible for his or her own orgasm.

Another rule they established is that they talk about sex, parenting issues, any kind of anger between them, problems at work, and other major issues outside the bedroom. I found it interesting that they were able to establish such rules for setting boundaries and establishing guidelines for implementing policies they had agreed on. Kendall became concerned, for example, that when his twelve-year-old son and ten-year-old daughter spent the weekend with them, everyone would be so busy that the four would not have a chance to sit down together. A house rule was established that before the children left to return to their mother, everyone would meet to talk about whatever issues arose during the weekend and to clear up any feelings that resulted.

It is evident that this relationship describes the mutual interactions of two adults and is not structured by the characteristics of adult children. Fear of people, obsessive approval seeking, and self-alienation are issues that Candy and Kendall have learned to resolve. Any difficulties they may have had with fun and intimacy have been replaced by the ability to feel and share their lives joyfully. They can activate the adult within themselves to communicate and share responsibility, the inner child to play, and the parent to establish rules for living.

Overcoming her fear of expressing her neediness to a man, rooted as it was in her relationship with her father, took Candy six years of hard work in recovery to accomplish. Compared to that, she found setting boundaries in the workplace to be relatively easy. As the manager of a newly opened shop, Candy found it necessary to establish boundaries with the woman who owns the business as to her working hours and responsibilities. Worried because the new business was not making money, the owner told Candy that her husband wanted to close out the shop. Candy replied that she needed to know how many hours a week she would be employed and whether the woman intended to sign another six-month lease for the shop. "I need to know that," she said. "I have other responsibilities in my life." Candy was able to mind her own business rather than get drawn into the owner's whirlpool of anxiety. In situations that involved other employees, she found it beneficial to give her boss similarly straightforward answers that clearly delineated their respective responsibilities.

Candy showed a willingness to take risks in relating to her friends and to Kendall's friends. When organizing a birthday party for him, for example, she told the people she invited, some of whom she did not know personally, that it was important to her to know whether they were going to attend or not. She felt that such assertiveness was risky when compared to her former pattern of placating everyone. She talked with her girlfriend to resolve her friend's feelings of jealousy for the time Candy was spending with her brother. She continued to work on taking care of herself with healthy nutrition, exercise, companionship, and a manageable work environment. "I won't work around smoke or abusive people," she said. These practices were further indications that her priority was to continue to develop her self-loving identity, and that her relationship with Kendall served to enhance her ability to be herself.

"I've been in recovery for seven years," she stated, "and the longer I do it the more natural it gets. I would go through all the pain of my childhood and early recovery again to be where I am today. There's a whole other side to all the pain." Her commitment to recovery has grown to encompass all aspects of her life. She continued to attend support group meetings and to connect with people. She considered therapy a resource available to her whenever she needed it, and was working with a therapist to better understand issues arising from her relationship with Kendall. "I like working on myself," she said. "It's like a fun research project."

Finally, expressing what could be a slogan for the self-actualizing spirit of genesis, she stated, "I'm creating every-thing that I'm living, and that's who I am." Candy stated that she sometimes still feels fear of people, and such feelings can be attributed to her wounded inner child. But this part of her continues to receive her own loving parenting, supported by people with whom she chooses to associate. For the most part she is comfortable and involved with people and author-ity figures, loves to be with people who love and take care of themselves, and is becoming ever more free to feel and express all her feelings.

Al

At the age of thirty-seven, Al has been married for fourteen years and continues to live with his wife and two children, a twelve-year-old son and nine-year-old daughter. His marriage has proved to be an exception to the rule for people in recov-ery. What happens most frequently is that one spouse in a marriage enters recovery while the other does not, and even-tually they grow apart. Occasionally both spouses become active in recovery, and work on their relationship from both ends. Such was the case with Al.

His own childhood had been chaotic, filled with the violence of a father who beat his mother. She, in turn, had no time or energy for Al and left him to fend for himself. She would tell him, for example, that it was important for him to attend school, but did nothing expected of a parent to help him get there. Her anger was sporadic and unpredictable, as she lashed out at Al to punish him for something that was okay the day before. Consequently, he strove to avoid painful aban-donment feelings by people-pleasing behaviors and by nurtur-ing himself with what was ever available, food.

"Caretaking became a form of addiction to satisfy my need of wanting to belong," he explained. "You can always belong if you are taking care of someone. That person will always want you in his or her life. I held on to that for decades." In his marriage he expressed this by buying things to cheer up his wife when she felt despondent. If she felt upset, he might buy her a new coat or a new ring. Once he tried to cheer her up by buying her a new car, a definite strain on his income as an auto accident insurance adjuster.

Redefining his identity in a relationship with a fourteen-year history has proved difficult for Al. He stated that he could not have succeeded to the point he has without the ACOA recovery program, personal and family therapy, and a facilitated therapy group. At the time I interviewed him he had been in recovery for four years and had invested thousands of dollars in the process.

The key to Al's relationship with his wife at the time I interviewed him was his reliance on his feelings, and his commitment to be honest with himself and with her about what they told him. Al described how this commitment worked in their relationship.

He recalled a day he and his wife had spent together after hiring a babysitter. They enjoyed the day visiting museums together, eating out, and playing board games with friends in the evening. Throughout the day they had engaged in touching, holding hands, and sexual teasing that set a mood of anticipation for the lovemaking that awaited them later. When Al sensed something was amiss during dinner his wife told him she had a headache, but that she had some aspirin to take and would be all right. But when they were getting ready for bed and Al invited her to engage in sex, she refused, again saying she had a headache. "Did you take the aspirin?" he asked. "No, I forgot," she said. Al felt very hurt, disappointed, and disregarded. An angry voice within him urged him to sleep on the couch. *Stay with your feelings,* he said to himself, *and then we can talk about it.* He went to sleep feeling sad.

The next morning he was awakened by his wife kissing and feeling him. *No, wait a minute,* he thought, *it's going to be real easy to get sexually excited and say that everything was fine last night.* "Do you want to fool around?" she asked. *If my wife asks me to fool around and I refuse, then she'll never ask me again,* said an old tape in his mind. *You have to be true to yourself,* he thought, *and put your disappointment out.* "No," Al said in response to her question. "I have some strong feelings about what happened last night, and I need to clear those up before I can be fully present today to make love with you."

Difficult as it was to let her see his vulnerability and how her behavior had hurt him, Al shared his feelings "rather than put on a stoic macho mask." He let her know it was not okay to lead him on all day and then say "No" so he would feel abandoned and disregarded. She responded by taking responsibility for her part in what had happened, and said she was sorry and had not meant to hurt him. They then made love, and the sex they shared was all the more satisfying because of their clear communication of feelings. "It was great," said Al, "and we had a really nice day."

It is evident from this transaction that Al first listened to his feelings, considered the pleadings of his wounded inner child to seek approval by people-pleasing behavior, and then dialogued with himself before communicating with his wife. Thus when he talked to her it was with a full consciousness of his feelings, thoughts, and desires. He could be, as he put it, "fully present" to the moment. In describing his relationship with his wife, Al provided a good definition of intimacy: "The relationship I have with her is based on mutual support, caring for each other, and allowing each other to have whatever feelings we have, without having to fix her, or have her fix me. I share my feelings and vulnerabilities with her, and am honest with what's going on for me. I take risks."

Al stated that had he denied his feelings of being disregarded, the pain would have stayed inside him, and he would have acted out his denial by overeating. At the time I interviewed Al, he had reduced his weight by about one hundred pounds from when I first met him two years before. Having struggled with weight all his life, he attributed his success in slimming down to a change in attitude. From being arrogant about how easy it was to lose weight, he had changed to admitting that it was indeed a hard thing to do.

He was participating in a weight clinic's program, and did what it took to keep himself faithful to the "rigidly regulated starch intake" the program required. For example, the program allowed only two slices of low-calorie bread a day, enough for one sandwich. But Al had always eaten two sandwiches for lunch and could not be satisfied with eating one. To satisfy himself he spent fifteen minutes every workday morning toasting the two slices of bread, carefully slicing them vertically into two slices each, using the filling for one sandwich for two sandwiches, and, because the sandwiches were too frail to carry in a baggie, carefully wrapping them in aluminum foil. Thus, at lunchtime he had the calories of one sandwich with the visual impact of two. "Doing this kind of work changes how I feel about myself," he said. "No one else can do this for me but me. It makes me feel honest. This is really hard, but I can stay on this food plan and reach my ultimate goal of being slim."

The feeling of self-worth Al got from doing this kind of thing is what he brought to his relationships with friends, new and old, his coworkers, and others. Because his sister and mother continued to relate to him abusively, disregarding his feelings and acting out the rage of repressed anger with him, he decided to stop visiting or calling them. The accounts he gave of interacting with his male friends resembled his interactions with his wife in terms of dialoguing honestly with himself and them.

"I have significant relationships with men where I can go out and be exactly who I am," he said. One time he spent a day with an old friend and a new person they were befriending, and he felt jealous when the other two went off to play golf for a while. *I had better not say anything about it,* an inner voice stated, *I'm just starting to have a relationship with this new guy.* But his feelings were clear. He was afraid his old friend would forget him now that he had someone new to play golf with. Al decided to take the risk and say how he felt.

"I feel really jealous," he said to his friend, "because we always played golf together, and now I feel I'm not going to be enough for you anymore. I'm afraid I'm not going to be part of your life, and that I'm going to be replaced by this other guy." "I hear you," his friend replied, "and I want to support you in that you're still part of my life." Al was pleased to hear this, but even more pleased with himself for taking the risk of sharing his vulnerability with a male friend.

In his therapy group Al found occasion to assert his needs and take a stand to see that they were met. His experiences in group therapy allow him the support to continue to grow and to understand better how to relate to people. It would be a misunderstanding of the recovery process to believe that once you reach genesis you no longer need therapy and support group meetings. On the contrary, both Candy and Al view these supports as resources to be utilized for their further growth. Genesis, while representing the last stage in the recovery process, signifies the beginning of your own life as an adult.

All of Al's dedication and commitment carry over to his relating with others, including his manager and coworkers. When he was asked to change his scheduled vacation time he explained why he could not do so. When, a few days before his vacation was to start, he was asked to take on additional work in another district, he said he was willing to do so as long as the manager decided which work he wanted Al to do. That is, Al was not going to work overtime and drive hundreds of extra miles to do both his regular work and the work from the adjoining district.

The boundaries Al set on his job were reasonable, and he asserted them in a spirit of cooperation rather than rebellion. They were recognized as such by his manager. Al had a ten-year history with his company and, in the past, had often rescheduled his vacations to please his boss or done extra work for no compensation. No longer driven by the obsessive need for approval, he found that relying on his feelings and stating his needs worked very well in changing his old role of the exploited victim to that of the employee who knows his value to the company and asserts his worthiness for due consideration. "No longer do I have to be the superworker," Al said. "I know my limitations, work within them, and take responsibility for that."

Al ended his interview with a very positive assessment of

himself. "I'm at a point in my recovery where I really have a great life," he said. This includes a warm relationship with his children, who relate to him with a trust and affection that was unknown in his family of origin. "I have some very significant intimate relationships with both men and women that are based on love, caring, understanding, support, and acceptance of each other. No one gets the right to abuse me, no matter what their role is in my life. I stand up for that very firmly, and have good boundaries today. I exercise, take good care of myself, and am committed to the recovery program."

At that point in his life Al was grieving the alienation he had experienced as a child after bonding with his mother and father during the first six months of his life. This process empowered him to be open to bonding with other people without being constantly on guard that they might hurt him. He realized that there was always the possibility of getting hurt, but that he had the skills to deal with that and take care of himself. As a result he was feeling the joy of experiencing from other people the love that he had lost in childhood.

Conclusion

Healing the wounds of childhood is not easy, but the rewards are well worth the effort. When compared to the alternative experience of continued deepening despair, isolation from meaningful contact with others, and the bitterness of self-alienation, there is no question that recovery is worth the pain. Those of us who have traveled thus far on their journey have no fear of regressing to earlier dysfunctions. They value the hard-won maturity of adulthood, the emotional freedom of their inner child, and the guidance of their inner parent. They have experienced real transformations in their personalities, in accordance with the natural laws of growth and development, and find their power in their understanding and respect for these natural laws.

Letting go of the magical thinking that helped you survive a childhood of abuse and neglect allows you to open yourself to the real magic of life. For there is magic in the changes of seasons that take place on this lovely planet, in the infinite variety and abundance of its living things, in the potential for growth and transformations offered by human life, and in the warmth with which people instinctively reach out to help and support one another. From sunrise to sunset the laws of nature, whether described by the physical, sociological, economic, psychological, or natural sciences, are framed in their own inexorable beauty. Living in accord with these laws is the art that all of us is challenged to learn, whether or not our families were dysfunctional. Living as a worthy human being is the highest form of art we can know.

THE 12 STEPS OF A.A.

(1). We admitted we were powerless over alcohol—that our lives had become unmanageable. (2). We came to believe that a power greater than ourselves could restore us to sanity. (3). We made a decision to turn our will and our lives over to the care of God *as we understood Him.* (4). We made a searching and fearless moral inventory of ourselves. (5). We admitted to God, to ourselves, and to another human being the exact nature of our wrongs. (6). We were entirely ready to have God remove all these defects of character. (7). We humbly asked Him to remove our shortcomings. (8). We made a list of all persons we had harmed, and became willing to make amends to them all. (9). We made direct amends to such people wherever possible, except when to do so would injure them or others. (10). We continued to take personal inventory and when we were wrong promptly admitted it. (11). We sought through prayer and meditation to improve our conscious contact with God *as we understood Him,* praying only for knowledge of His will for us and the power to carry that out. (12). Having had a spiritual awakening as a result of these steps, we tried to carry this message to alcoholics, and to practice these principles in all our affairs.

BIBLIOGRAPHY

Augustine Fellowship. *Sex and Love Addicts Anonymous.* Boston: Fellowship Wide Services, 1987.

Barker, Philip, MB. *Basic Child Psychiatry.* Baltimore: University Park Press, 1979.

Beattie, Melody. *Codependent No More.* Hazelden, Box 176, Center City, MN, 55012-0176, 1987.

Berne, Eric, M.D. *Games People Play.* New York: Ballantine Books, 1964.

Brown, Stephanie. *Treating the Alcoholic: A developmental model of recovery.* New York: John Wiley & Sons, 1985.

Brownmiller, Susan. "Madly in Love." *Ms.,* April 1989, pp. 56ff.

Brozan, Nadine. "Unresolved Issue: Is Nussbaum Culpable?", *New York Times,* Jan. 24, 1989, p. B1.

Carnes, Patrick, Ph.D. *Out of the Shadows; Understanding Sexual Addiction,* Minneapolis: CompCare Publishers, 1983.

Cermak, Timmen L., M.D. *A Primer on Adult Children of Alcoholics.* Health Communications. Enterprise Center, 3201 S.W. 15th Street, Deerfield Beach, Fla., 1985.

Desai, Yogi Amrit. *Kripalu Yoga: Meditation-in-Motion.* Lenox, Mass.: Kripalu Publications, 1981.

———. *Kripalu Yoga: Meditation-in-Motion, Book II.* Lenox, Mass.: Kripalu Publications, 1985.

Erikson, Erik H. *Childhood and Society.* 2nd ed. New York: W. W. Norton, 1963.

Fields, Rick, with Peggy Taylor, Rex Weyler, and Rick Ingrasci. *Chop Wood Carry Water: A Guide to Finding Spiritual Fulfillment in Everyday Life.* Los Angeles: Jeremy P. Tarcher, 1984.

Friends in Recovery. *The 12 Steps: A Way Out.* San Diego: Recovery Publications, 1987.

————. *The 12 Steps for Adult Children.* San Diego: Recovery Publications, 1987.

Goldman, Albert. *Elvis.* New York: McGraw-Hill, 1981.

Gorsky, Terry. "ACOA Relationships." Speech given at the Convention of the National Association of Adult Children of Alcoholics, San Diego, CA. February 13, 1988.

Gravitz, Herbert L., and Julie D. Bowden. *Guide to Recovery: A book for ACOAs.* Holmes Beach, Fla.: Learning Publications Inc., 1985.

Gross, Ken. "Denying his guilt, Joel Steinberg tells how he cared for the child he killed and the lover he beat." *People,* March 13, 1989, pp. 71ff.

Halpern, Howard M., Ph.D. *How to Break Your Addiction to a Person.* New York: Bantam Books, 1982.

Hay, Louise L. *You Can Heal Your Life.* Santa Monica: Hay House, 1984.

Leaming, Barbara. *Orson Welles: A Biography.* New York: Viking-Penguin, 1983.

Maeder, Thomas. "Wounded Healers." *Atlantic Monthly,* January 1989, pp. 37–47.

McCabe, Robert J. R. "Alcohol-Dependent Individuals Sixteen Years On." *Alcohol and Alcoholism* 21 (1986): 85–91.

Missildine, W. Hugh, M.D. *Your Inner Child of the Past.* New York: Pocket Books, 1963.

Peck, M. Scott, M.D. *The Road Less Traveled.* New York: Simon & Schuster, 1978.

———. *People of the Lie.* New York: Simon & Schuster, 1983.

Roban, Arleen. "Domestic Violence and Alcohol: Barriers to Cooperation." *Alcohol Health and Research World,* Winter 1985–86, pp. 22–27.

Rothberg, Neil M., M.A. "The Alcoholic Spouse and the Dynamics of Co-Dependency." *Alcoholism Treatment Quarterly* 3 (Spring 1986): 73–86.

Schaeffer, Brenda. *Is it Love or Is It Addiction?* San Francisco: Harper/Hazelden, 1987.

Seixas, Judith S., and Geraldine Youcha. *Children of Alcoholism: A Survivor's Manual.* New York: Crown, 1985.

Siegel, Bernie S. *Love, Medicine and Miracles.* New York: Harper & Row, 1986.

Simmons, Judy. "Out of Bounds." *Ms.,* April 1989, pp. 65ff.

Steiner, Claude. *Games Alcoholics Play.* New York: Ballantine Books, 1971.

Suh, Mary. "Understanding Battered Women." *Ms.,* April 1989, p. 62.

Summers, Anne. "The Hedda Conundrum." *Ms.,* April 1989, p. 54.

Wegscheider, Sharon. *Another Chance: Hope and Health for the Alcoholic Family.* Palo Alto: Science and Behavior Books, 1981.

Wegscheider-Cruse, Sharon. *Choice-Making: For Co-Dependents, Adult Children, and Spirituality Seekers.* Pompano Beach, Fla.: Health Communications, 1985.

Whitfield, Charles L. *Healing the Child Within.* Pompano Beach, Fla.: Health Communications, 1987.

Woititz, Janet Geringer. *Adult Children of Alcoholics.* Pompano Beach, Fla.: Health Communications, 1983.